Elegant Leadership:
Simple Strategies, Remarkable Results

Andrew Neitlich

Chatham Business Press
San Anselmo, CA

Elegant Leadership:

Simple Strategies, Remarkable Results

By Andrew Neitlich

Published by Chatham Business Press
San Anselmo, California

Publisher's Cataloging-in-Publication
(Provided by Quality Books, Inc.)

Neitlich, Andrew.
Elegant leadership : simple strategies, remarkable results / Andrew Neitlich. -- 1st ed.
p. cm.
Includes bibliographical references.
LCCN: 2001095816
ISBN: 0-9714708-0-4

1. Leadership. 2. Executive ability. I. Title.

HD57.7.N45 2002 658.4'092
QBI01-201207

Praise for Elegant Leadership

"The wisdom contained within the pages of *Elegant Leadership* comprises the kind of practical learnings most managers are unable to master in a lifetime of practice. Andrew Neitlich has produced a user's guide to outstanding performance...a must read and more importantly, a must do!"

- Len Schlesinger, Executive Vice President and Chief Operating Officer, The Limited, Inc.

"Leaders are often advised to look at themselves in the mirror. This book suggests what they should be looking for and what to do about what they see. *Elegant Leadership* is a leader's companion—practical advice presented in an actionable form for people who rarely get either."

- James Heskett, co-author, *The Service Profit Chain*

"*Elegant Leadership* is a simple, clear blueprint to value-based leadership in today's increasingly competitive business environment. It takes the reader back to basics and reminds him to create the future using a principled, high-touch approach that is badly needed in our high-tech world. Andrew Neitlich elegantly and insightfully describes a set of simple, powerful, practical, and even graceful personal leadership strategies that should be required reading for all executives."

- Scott Durchslag, former Partner, McKinsey & Company

"Andrew is one of the most knowledgeable and passionate experts on leadership that I have ever known—this is an opportunity to save yourself a lot of effort by getting the most relevant, up-to-date insights distilled for you by a truly brilliant thought leader in his own right."

- Andrew Bein, Vice President/General Manager, Digital Business Group, Reader's Digest

"Andrew Neitlich is brilliant! Truly a master executive coach! His ability to guide company management through a mass of complex decisions is exceptional, and his outstanding advice results in dramatically increased leadership productivity."

- Susan Dworak, Founder and President, Exponential Training

Praise for Elegant Leadership

"In a world of business experts, Andrew Neitlich stands out, in large measure, because of his ability to quickly analyze complex business situations...and immediately see a clear path to solid results. Every...executive needs an Andrew Neitlich to help him or her discern the forest from the trees."

- Harley Christensen, Founder, The Evergreen Project

"Andrew has a rare gift for distilling the essential elements of effective management into a clear, step-by-step approach that ensures outstanding achievements for leaders in any organization. He asks the kind of questions that inspire visionary thinking coupled with practical steps to achieving results. I recommend his work for anyone interested in a streamlined, no nonsense approach to building teams and breakaway performance."

- Peter Meyers, Founder and Executive Director, Vector Theater Conservatory

"Management books written by consultants generally focus on improving performance to achieve profit goals. Often the social capital of a corporation is neglected. What makes Neitlich's book invaluable is the way that he joins these two elements thus helping the manager to simultaneously improve the bottom line while enhancing employee satisfaction."

**- Nancy McAward, Chief Operating Officer and Chief Nursing Officer,
St. Thomas Hospital, Nashville**

"Andrew has secured a solid position as an expert on leadership theory and practice."

- Suzie Pollak, President, Marin Nexus

For my clients

Table of Contents

Acknowledgements

This book is based on more than a decade of practice, research, study, and observation. Therefore, I am indebted to literally thousands of people who have shown me what it means to lead elegantly (and not).

However, a few people deserve special recognition. First, a number of clients and colleagues have been extremely generous in their willingness to let me test new ideas with them, and to learn from their leadership style: *Larry Barton, Jeanne Bogardus, Marsha Bonner, Harley Christensen, Susan Dworak, Elissa Giambastiani, Susan Gilmore, Chris Van Gorder, Mike Groza, Carolyn Horan, Deborah Levy, Lawland Long, Peter Meyers, Ron Mogel, Paul Morrell, Dr. Thomas Peters, Suzie Pollak, Veronica Reed, Robert Reitherman, Bruce Truitt, Dave Wilson, Jonathan Wilson, and John Wilson-Bugbee.*

Second, many teachers, mentors, and managers along the way have taught me valuable lessons about how to lead more elegantly: *David Alger, David Anderson, Nancy Buttenheim, Frank Calderon, Jonathan Foust, James Heskett, Dr. Ian Kadish, Colleen Kohler, Grant Lasson, Tony Merlo, Dan Robinson, Tom Rose, George Sauter, Len Schlesinger, Mona Sowiski, John Steinberg, and Mike Wilbur.*

As for direct support for the book, I am grateful that I found *Jessica Williams* of *Spark Design (www.sparkdesign.cc)*, who designed the book from cover to cover. I am also grateful that *Courtney Benvenuti* of *Courtney Benvenuti Communications*, who edited and refined most of the sentences in the book, lives nearby.

Finally, I wish to express enormous gratitude to my wife *Elena*, who provided support while I worked weekends and late into the night. She is an elegant friend, spouse, coach, and partner.

Introduction

The purpose of this book is to significantly raise the standards by which we judge and measure leaders. Today, the word *leadership* is almost meaningless. We tell workers to display leadership by having a good attitude and showing up on time. We call training in basic supervisory skills "leadership."

And when people do exert leadership, they are often sloppy about it. Many sacrifice relationships. Some compromise ethics. Others exhibit all sorts of disagreeable behaviors. Still others fail to think rigorously about the right strategy or course of action. We excuse this sloppiness by arguing that results justify the means.

"Elegant leadership" tolerates neither watered-down definitions of leadership, nor sloppiness. In this book, leadership means creating a significantly better future than would have been possible without a leader. A good leader creates something out of nothing, and the results are significant. And the leader matters: without his or her contribution, results would not have been nearly as impressive.

There are four essential ways in which an elegant leader creates the future:

> ***1. Simply.*** Elegant leaders distill infinite information and possibilities into the one or two essential elements that will make the largest difference. Their speech, thinking, and actions all reflect simplicity.
>
> ***2. Powerfully.*** Simplicity alone is superficial. Elegant leaders create the future in simple ways that also have power. Like the lever in basic physics, elegant leaders find ways to have a huge impact with minimal force.
>
> ***3. Practically.*** Elegant leaders are not dreamers, or academics. They live in the real world, take action, and focus on what will work. An elegant leader will implement an 80 percent solution, or make decisions with 60 percent of the information he or she wants, in order to move things forward in a practical way.
>
> ***4. Gracefully.*** Elegant leaders do their work with refinement. They are consummate professionals, simultaneously strengthening relationships while moving toward their goals. They maintain impeccable character, and remain resilient in good times and bad.

The Four Attributes of Elegant Leadership:

Simple

Powerful

Practical

Graceful

Why lead elegantly? Because by leading elegantly, you will get better results in less time, with stronger professional relationships, and with greater personal and professional fulfillment.

This book provides simple, powerful, practical, and graceful strategies and tools to help you lead elegantly. It offers frameworks, worksheets, questions, and assessments that will help you clarify your thinking, expand your skills, and get better responses from your colleagues. Each chapter focuses on a different aspect of elegant leadership. Depending on your interests, you may focus on one, some, or all, of the chapters. They include:

Get grounded. This chapter provides a one-page dashboard that clearly defines your mission, vision, goals, key initiatives, key relationships, and opportunities for continued development. With this dashboard in hand, you can focus on what really matters in chaotic times.

Wipe your feet at the door. You will be challenged to eliminate disagreeable, unproductive, career-limiting behaviors by completing *The Survey No One Wants to Take.*

Take care of your needs. Leaders have enough on their minds at work without having to focus on personal problems. This short chapter asks you to indulge your personal needs in order to find clarity, peace, and strength.

Cultivate the right attitude. Great leaders have great attitudes, mindsets, beliefs, and ways of being that lay the foundation for elegant leadership.

Develop an elegant strategy. While leaders build compelling visions of the future, they also develop powerful and practical strategies for getting there. This chapter suggests that the crux of strategy is determining what your organization should do best, in terms that matter to your customers and make your organization unique in the marketplace.

Communicate simply and powerfully. This chapter reminds leaders about listening and speaking authentically, about creating concise and compelling messages, and about expanding effective communication throughout your organization.

Strengthen your power base. Leaders depend on the quality of their professional relationships. This chapter offers a simple process for identifying and strengthening your most important professional relationships.

Engage and mobilize employees. Many of us could pay more attention to how we mobilize, lead, coach, and develop our employees. This chapter provides practical tools and strategies for understanding our employees and providing them with the support they need to succeed.

Elegant leadership from below. Most leaders report to somebody, whether another executive, the CEO, a board member, an investor, or customers. Since the manager is one of the most important people in the leader's power base, this chapter focuses exclusively on strengthening that relationship.

Think comprehensively. Many leadership pundits underestimate the importance of critical and comprehensive thinking. They assume that with enough vision and passion, leaders will get results. This chapter takes a contrary view, and argues that leaders absolutely must be able to think clearly, practically, and comprehensively.

Successfully influence others. Leaders succeed by influencing others to think, speak, and act differently. They do this in a way that simultaneously gets results and maintains relationships, without manipulating. This chapter provides tools, templates, and strategies to influence others elegantly.

Move things forward. Ultimately, leaders get results by moving things forward. This happens much more easily when leaders implement the strategies and tools elsewhere in this book. This chapter builds on preceding ones by providing specific tools for moving things toward a successful conclusion.

Foster collaboration. In authentic collaboration, all parties benefit. As this chapter shows, elegant leaders work hard to foster collaboration, both inside and outside their organizations.

Build for the future. Most executives have enough of a challenge achieving short-term results. This chapter helps you build an organization (or a piece of one) that will last longer than you do.

Give something back. Elegant leaders contribute beyond their organizations. They get involved with, and solve, issues of personal interest. They also find ways to promote their organization and develop emerging leaders by encouraging civic involvement.

One final note: This book is not for everyone—only leaders with courage and thick skin. It asks you to assess yourself honestly, ask others for advice, make difficult choices, and change ineffective behaviors.

As you read this book, please feel free to contact me with thoughts and feedback, or to share your stories of elegant leadership, at aneitlich@sagogroup.com. In the meantime, thank you for your willingness to raise the bar and lead elegantly.

Get Grounded

Leading an organization takes tremendous resilience, patience, and coping skills. How many crises do you address every day? How many requests for your time distract you from achieving your real goals and handling your primary responsibilities? How often do people in your organization ask you to do things that *they* should be doing?

Meanwhile, you probably face unprecedented pressures. Markets are changing more quickly. Customers demand more, and forgive less. Employees feel less loyalty. Competitors announce new breakthroughs in rapid time.

In this environment, it becomes enormously difficult to keep track of the few things that really matter: vision, mission, values, performance, relationships, and how to become more effective. If you are not careful, you can lose perspective and become scattered, when you really need to be grounded—focused, calm, resilient, and powerful.

This chapter provides a 10-step process to help you get and stay grounded. By the end, you will have a one-page plan, or "dashboard." This dashboard will tell you the direction to take your organization, why you should, and how.

The dashboard challenges you to clearly and simply state your ideas about seven essential areas:

Vision. It is important to have a simple and inspiring vision of where the organization is going. That way, when work pulls you in multiple directions you can keep perspective and prioritize.

Mission. In addition to having a vision, it is also important for you to know why you are doing what you are doing. What's the higher purpose for all of your hard work? How will the planet be better if you achieve your long-term vision? Why will it matter to you, and to others? By knowing the answer to those questions, you can remain grounded in purpose.

Values. Values play a key role in grounding leaders. When you find yourself under extreme pressure, values help you persevere and thrive—gracefully.

Performance. Ultimately, you are paid to perform. However, few executives can quickly and simply define what "performance" means to them. This section challenges you to choose the key measures that tell you whether you are doing a great job. That way, you can easily communicate what you need to do, and what you need others to do.

Initiatives. Many executives take on projects that bear little relationship to their performance goals or their vision. By carefully choosing a few projects with high impact, you can manage your time and improve results.

Professional relationships. Leaders get results by working with other people. Therefore, having strong professional relationships with the right people determines a large part of your success. This piece of the dashboard asks you to identify the key people you need on your side in order to succeed.

Development. Great leaders continuously evolve, learn, and improve. They build on strengths, adopt more effective behaviors, and learn new skills and knowledge. This section challenges you to choose the few areas where your development will lead directly to improved results.

It is not easy to remain grounded as a leader of a complex and evolving organization. The questions that follow require you to think, reflect, get advice from others, and prioritize. It may sound like a lot of work, but it is worth the effort. By being clear on your vision, mission, values, performance goals, and areas for development, you will remain calm and focused when others panic.

Take some time to review the dashboard below, and then complete each section in this chapter.

The Elegant Leader's Dashboard

Vision	What is your vision for the organization? What problem will your organization solve? What value does your organization add, and for which customers? With what products and services? Where? How? How big is the opportunity?
Mission	What higher good do you achieve through your work? For which aspect(s) of your work do you feel most passionate?
Values	What non-negotiable values, attributes and principles define how you work? How do your actions compare to the values you say are important to you?
Performance	What specific, measurable results define success for you on the job? Over what time frame?
Initiatives	Which projects and campaigns do you need to drive in order to achieve your vision and desired level of performance?
Professional relationships	Which colleagues are key to your success?
Development	Which of your strengths can you build on to succeed? Which behaviors do you need to change or adopt? What skills and knowledge do you need to acquire?

Craft a Long-Term Vision

A clear vision of where your organization is going provides leaders with focus and direction over time. A compelling vision can also inspire employees to go the extra mile.

This section challenges you to articulate a concise, clear and motivating vision of where you want to take your organization. Using the worksheet that follows, describe what your organization will look like in three to five years. Remember to state the future in the present tense, so that it becomes more concrete.

Worksheet: Vision

	In Three To Five Years?
What problem are you solving in the market?	
What products and services do you provide?	
What does your organization do better than any other? What is your organization famous for?	
Which types of customers does your organization serve? Which types doesn't it serve?	
What value does your organization provide for these customers? What is unique about the way in which you do business?	
Where is your organization located? Is your organization local, national, or international?	
What processes, technology, expertise, people, and systems facilitate your vision?	
How big can your organization get? What share of the market can it have?	
What are the key milestones you need to reach to achieve your vision? What major achievements will you celebrate along the way?	

With your completed Vision Worksheet, craft a vision statement that is compelling, inspiring, unique, and audacious—one that will get you out of bed in the morning. Later on, you will ask a couple of colleagues for feedback; for now, create the best draft of the statement that works for you. If you wish, use the examples below as templates.

Examples:

In five years, we are a wildly successful consulting company that helps executives become better leaders. Executives and human resource professionals from the most dynamic organizations in the nation call us first for executive coaching and customized training. We are famous for helping people make massive leaps in performance, and for our practical and powerful programs.

In five years, we are a highly respected carpet cleaning company that creates a professional, fresh, and appealing environment. We work for the largest property owners in California, including owners of the most prestigious hotels and office buildings. Our 300 employees own part of the company, and enjoy working here so much that our turnover is lowest in the industry. We are famous for being friendly, fast and impeccable.

In five years, we are a nationally recognized training and coaching firm, specializing in teaching managers how to speak publicly with power and humor. We are famous for transforming ordinary people into engaging and inspiring speakers. Publications including The Wall Street Journal *and* Barron's *have written about our unique approach to training. Executives from* Fortune 500 *companies pay up to $10,000 per day for individualized coaching on presentation skills. Our book is a bestseller. We have offices in San Francisco, Los Angeles, Chicago, New York, Boston and Atlanta.*

In five years, we are the industry standard with our patented solution for encrypting financial transactions over the Internet. We license our software to companies in twenty-five countries. We are a publicly traded company, with steady revenue and earnings growth. We attract the best software engineers in the industry, thanks to a culture that rewards performance, encourages innovation, and demands excellence.

Your vision statement:

What Is Your Mission?

Without a higher purpose, or passion for what they do, most leaders will not last. This is true for two reasons: First, without a mission that inspires them, they won't be able to survive the pressures of leading. Second, few people will follow leaders who aren't working toward a compelling and inclusive purpose.

What is your higher purpose, or mission, that helps you tolerate all of the chaos you face each day? The more compelling your purpose and the more passionate you are, the better your chances for sustained fulfillment—and the better the chances that employees and colleagues will follow your leadership.

Answer the questions in the following worksheet.

Worksheet: Mission

What are the selfish reasons you work? What ends can you achieve that bring you fulfillment?	
What are the higher reasons why you work? How are you making a positive difference in the world?	
About which aspects of your work are you most passionate?	

If you had trouble answering the last two questions in the worksheet, then answer these questions:

- Are your selfish motivations enough to keep you going as a leader?
- Will others find your selfish motivations inspiring enough to follow you?

If you can answer "yes" to both questions, then congratulations are in order. If not, then reconsider the importance of having some higher purpose in your work, and of contributing to something that you—and your colleagues—care about deeply.

Now, craft your answers to the above into a concise statement that will keep you going when times get rough.

My mission at work is:

Examples: *"I'm helping to feed the world."*
-Executive of an agricultural production company

"I want people to succeed in work and life."
-Printer of business cards and stationery

"I'm creating a world that is safe, hygienic, and healthy."
-Executive of a company that manufactures toilets

Know Which Values Matter Most to You

Values are principles and attributes that you hold dear. At work, values define not what you do, but how you do it. They define who you are while you work. Even when you feel extreme pressure and stress, you do not compromise your values. Values provide a set of principles that underlies everything you do. What are your values? Illustrative values include:

Have fun	*Respect people*	*Win*
Take risks	*Execute flawlessly*	*Embrace complexity*
Be compassionate	*Think*	*Strive for excellence*
Push the envelope	*Never give up*	*Be a slow, continuous force*
Delight the customer	*Have total integrity*	*Learn and improve*
Be resourceful	*Collaborate*	*See greatness in others*
Be consistent	*Innovate*	*Be faster to market*

There are two types of values: those that you say you have and put into action, and those that you say you have and *don't* put into action. If your actions don't match the values you claim to embrace, then you shouldn't call them your values. For instance, the CEO of a hospital claimed that one of his primary values was to respect every employee. Meanwhile, he tolerated surgeons who used abusive language with nurses. He also laid off five percent of his staff in a careless, callous way. Based on these actions, he wasn't upholding the values he claimed to have. In the worksheet that follows, list your four most important values, as well as specific evidence to prove that your actions match your intentions.

Worksheet: Values

Value	Specific Evidence (Actions That Prove This Is A Value)

Examples:

Have fun	*I lead a weekly awards ceremony with gag gifts and awards.* *I started a monthly potluck lunch event with staff.*
Strive for excellence	*I sacrificed $25,000 in revenue by delaying shipments until we could be sure quality met the highest standards in the industry.*

Take another look at your list. Would your closest colleagues agree that these are your values? Later in this chapter, you will have the chance to find out!

Define Performance

You earn the right to lead based on your ability to perform and get results. By having a clear picture of the results you must get, you can remain grounded. When crises hit, when competing priorities pull you in different directions, you can always focus by returning to your performance goals.

Performance goals are specific and measurable, and have a deadline. For instance, "Improve customer loyalty," is vague, can't be measured, and lacks a deadline. On the other hand, "Increase sales to each of our top ten customers by 20 percent over the next year," meets all three criteria.

How do you define performance for yourself? How do you know if you are doing a good job? Do you measure success primarily in terms of financial performance, market share, quality, customer satisfaction, employee development, productivity, innovation, speed, or some other metric? Whether you are a CEO or a front-line manager, performance should boil down to no more than three objectives. If you pick more than three, you will have a hard time focusing your efforts.

Choosing a few objectives is hard to do. It requires discipline and making tough decisions about your real priorities. To choose, think about the following question: What are the three most important criteria for your success? Put another way: What are the three areas of performance that—if you are not achieving them—will make you worry about keeping your job? Given your answers, complete the following worksheet:

Worksheet: Performance

My Top Three Performance Goals:

1.
2.
3.

Examples of the performance goals of the Executive Director of a theater school:

1. *Enroll 700 students in classes this year.*
2. *Sell 2,500 tickets to each performance this year.*
3. *Recruit 10 high schools that will offer our programs by June 30.*

Examples of the performance goals of the CEO of a software company:

1. *Increase revenue from $10 million to $13 million by the end of the year.*
2. *Develop and beta test two new software programs, one by July 31 and one by October 31.*
3. *Hire seven engineers in the next three months.*

Examples of the performance goals of a partner in a law firm:

1. *Create a new practice in real estate that generates $2 million by the end of the year.*
2. *Develop a retainer relationship with five of the 50 largest companies in the Bay Area.*
3. *Recruit five new partners by May 15.*

Choose Key Initiatives

Most of us have too many projects to complete. Worse, many of our projects do not directly and powerfully contribute to our performance goals or long-term vision. For instance, the CEO of a professional service firm had a single performance goal: Build a $1 billion organization through acquisitions. When he counted the projects that he supported or led, he found to his amazement that he spent his time on over 50 projects! These projects ranged from new product development to new employee orientation and compensation management—not to mention client work.

After realizing that few of his projects were actually helping him achieve his primary performance objective, he refocused his attention on three initiatives: identifying acquisition targets, evaluating acquisition targets, and completing successful acquisitions. He delegated—or postponed—everything else. As a result, he focused his time much more effectively, and also helped develop other leaders in his organization.

Most of us can focus on about three projects at a time. Which three projects—either new initiatives or ongoing—will help you achieve your performance goals and/or long-term vision over the next year? The worksheet below has room for more than three projects to allow you to list projects that will start when others finish.

Worksheet: Key Projects and Initiatives

Project Description	Start/ End Date	Outcomes	How The Project Supports Your Goals And/Or Vision

Given your answers above:

Which projects will you cancel or postpone in order to focus your attention?

Which projects will you delegate to others in your organization?

Identify Important Professional Relationships

Leaders rely on all sorts of people, in all sorts of roles, to achieve their vision and performance goals: colleagues, mentors, customers, managers, direct reports, and outside advisors. These people provide value in different ways, from knowledge and resources to support.

Developing strong professional relationships with as many people as possible represents a worthy goal. However, a small number of the people in your Rolodex have a disproportionate say about whether you succeed or not. By identifying and nurturing these key relationships, you can increase your chances of success while focusing your time and attention.

The worksheet below provides a simple tool for identifying the relationships that you absolutely must develop and maintain. List up to 20 people who play a vital role in helping you achieve your vision and goals.

Worksheet: Key Relationships

Role	Names	How They Can Help Me Succeed
Peers and colleagues		
Mentors		
Customers		
Managers		
Direct reports		
Investors		
Outside advisors		
Other key people		

Pick Areas for Professional Development

Leaders continuously improve and evolve to achieve their ambitious goals. Consider your vision, mission, values, and performance goals. What will it take for you to succeed? What strengths can you build on? What behaviors will you have to adopt or modify? What knowledge or skills will you have to acquire?

If your answer is "none," then go back and set some more challenging goals, or create a more outrageous vision. When you feel comfortable that your goals and vision are a stretch for you, fill in the following worksheets:

Think about your strengths. List one to three strengths that you can build upon to achieve your goals and vision.

Worksheet: Strengths

Strength	How It Supports My Goals And/Or Vision	How I Can Build On This Strength To Be Even More Effective

List one to three behaviors that you can change to achieve your performance goals and vision.

Worksheet: Behaviors

Old Behavior	How This Behavior Keeps Me From Attaining My Goals And/Or Vision	New Behavior: "I will..."

List three skills or areas of knowledge you need to acquire to be successful.

Worksheet: Knowledge

Skill/Area Of Knowledge	How It Will Help Me Achieve My Goals And/Or Vision	How/When I Will Develop It

Draft an Initial Plan

You now have substantial data. Using your work so far, draft an initial dashboard by filling in the template that follows. See the final, completed plan at the end of this chapter for an example.

Remember, this template represents only a draft. Your next step will be to get feedback from others.

Draft: The Elegant Leader's Dashboard

Vision	
Mission	
Values	
Performance	
Initiatives	
Professional relationships *(List names of key people)*	
Development	

Get Feedback

You now have a draft dashboard to help you get grounded. Before you conclude that this plan is accurate and compelling, check with people that you respect. Others often see aspects of ourselves that we may overlook.

Choose five people who work closely with you. Show them your draft dashboard. Get their feedback about your dashboard by asking the following questions.

Survey for Feedback On Your Draft Dashboard

Vision	Is my vision compelling to you? Have I taken it far enough? How can it be more compelling? How would other executives in the organization react to it? How would front-line staff react to it?
Mission	Does this mission statement seem authentic given what you know about me? How does this fit with the mission of the company? How compelling is this mission to you?
Values	Based on my actions, how would you define my values? Based on my actions, do I embrace the values I've chosen? How can I more closely bring these values to my work? How do these values relate to our company's values?
Performance	Are these goals the right performance goals for me to succeed? Am I stretching far enough? Is each goal specific and measurable? Relevant? Will these performance goals help me achieve the above vision?
Initiatives	Are these the three projects that you would choose to help me achieve my performance goals and vision? Do they tie closely enough to my definition of performance, and to what it will take to achieve the vision? Can you suggest any other, more relevant initiatives? Are the outcomes specific enough?
Professional relationships	Who do you think are the key people I need on my side in order to succeed? Are the people I have listed the right people? How would you assess my relationships with the people that you know on this list? What advice would you offer to strengthen these relationships?
Development	What behaviors do you think I need to change, or adopt, to achieve my performance goals? To achieve my vision? What strengths do I have that will help me reach my goals? How can I build on those? What do you think are the key skills and areas of knowledge I need to develop to succeed? What other advice would you offer to help me achieve these performance goals and this vision?

Finalize the Plan

With your colleagues' feedback in hand, finalize your dashboard. Keep this document on your desk, in your pocket—anywhere accessible. Anytime that you feel stressed, or pulled in too many directions, refer to it. It will help you focus on what really matters (at least at work).

Future sections of this book will dig deeper into each of these areas. As you finish the book, you may find yourself revising your dashboard. In the meantime, the version you have just completed provides a terrific way to stay grounded.

An example of a completed dashboard may look something like this:

Example: The Elegant Leader's Dashboard

Vision	To create an executive coaching and consulting business that becomes nationally recognized for its ability to help CEOs change their behavior and improve their performance—with a simple and powerful process.
Mission	Work becomes a source of fulfillment for everyone. People achieve goals they never thought possible.
Values	Be passionate. Be curious. Serve everyone I can.
Performance	In the next year, build a base of at least 20 paying clients and revenue of at least $750,000. In the year after, have 35 clients and be so busy that I can hire another consultant.
Initiatives	Publish a book by October. Find 20 complementary firms who will exchange referrals by October. Identify and join five associations by June.
Professional relationships	Each and every client I meet; Joe Davis; Bob Jones; Elena Marie; Jim Moore; Ed Levy; John Smith; Susan Robinson; and Mark Lee.
Development	I will learn about how to publish and market a book. I will be less modest about my talents and expertise, and evangelize what I do to everyone! In the next year I will learn at least two new assessment tools to use in my practice.

The Elegant Leader's Dashboard

Vision	
Mission	
Values	
Performance	
Initiatives	
Professional relationships	
Development	

Wipe Your Feet at the Door

At a children's theater school in my community, teachers remind students that, when they come to rehearsals, they need to "wipe their feet at the door." The expression means that they leave any and all nasty behaviors behind. No swearing, no fighting, no whining, no gossiping, and no criticizing other students.

As adults, many of us could improve our performance and relationships by wiping our feet at the door. As successful as we are, many of us still behave in ways that don't work. Some of us have become arrogant, dismissive of others, haughty, controlling, rigid, and defensive. Others have gone to the opposite extreme. For instance, we may avoid conflict to remain popular, delay important decisions, or tolerate lack of accountability.

Our success can enable these behaviors in two ways. First, as we achieve more and more, we may assume that we are smarter or better than our colleagues. We dismiss others' ideas, and become impatient with those who think differently than we do. Second, we tend to rely on the strategies and behaviors that helped us become successful; but, unfortunately, many of these strengths become weaknesses as we take on new challenges and roles. For instance, a reliance on teamwork and consensus may help to grow a company, but could create problems during a crisis that requires immediate action.

Even if we behave effectively on routine days, we are still prone to inappropriate behavior when days become stressful. As biologists have discovered, people react two ways when they face stress: some fight, while others flee or freeze. People who fight appear aggressive, abusive, coercive, and arrogant. People who flee or freeze appear to be passive/aggressive, weak, unwilling to face difficult issues, and unable to make tough decisions.

Few executives enjoy discovering that some of their behaviors alienate others, hurt morale, decrease productivity, stifle open communication, and compromise an organization's values. Fewer still are willing to change their approach and their behaviors. After all, why change what has been working? If doggedness built the company, why can't the same quality take the company to the next level?

Hard as it may be to change, there is no excuse for disagreeable behavior. This chapter challenges you to discover—and change—behaviors that don't work. It focuses on the behaviors that can really hurt your career and your organization if you don't change them soon.

Because adults have had more time than children to reinforce bad habits, and because they are generally more stubborn, most adults need a little more time than children to wipe their feet at the door.

Wiping your feet at the door requires four steps:

Become aware of behaviors you want to change.

Set goals for new behavior(s).

Get advice and clear up past mistakes.

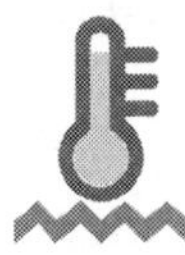

Measure progress and follow up.

If you follow these four simple steps, you will reap some enormous benefits with only a modest investment of time. First, you will eliminate the behaviors that cause many executives to fail. Second, you will strengthen relationships by repairing the past and involving others in your quest to improve.

Not everyone is willing to go through this powerful, foolproof process. Many claim that they don't have time, that things will get better on their own, that they can live with their shortcomings. Others lack the will to elicit honest feedback. This process is not for everyone—only leaders who want to build the strongest organization possible, form the most solid relationships, and have the most fulfilling careers.

Become Aware of Behaviors

The first step is one of the hardest. It takes courage to ask for feedback on behaviors that may be hurting relationships and performance. This section provides a tool that will help ease this process. It is called *The Survey No One Wants to Take*. There are two versions, one abridged and one unabridged, included on the following pages for easy photocopying and distribution. Are you willing to complete it? If not, that already gives you information about one habit you might want to change.

To maintain confidentiality and encourage people to answer honestly, consider asking a neutral party to administer the survey. Ask at least five colleagues that have worked closely with you to participate. Each colleague should indicate how often he or she has seen you display the behaviors listed. You should also complete the survey yourself to compare how you assess your behaviors with the way others see you. If you want to include additional behaviors, you are encouraged to modify the survey.

Turn to the survey on the next page. 

For: ______________________________
Your Name Here

The Survey No One Wants to Take (Unabridged Version)

Behavior	Frequency Of Each Behavior				
	Never	Rarely	Sometimes	Often	Always
Abdicates responsibility by not providing support, tools, coaching, or direction when needed.	○	○	○	○	○
Prefers being popular to getting results; avoids constructive conflict to keep peace.	○	○	○	○	○
Is arrogant.	○	○	○	○	○
Relies on an autocratic, controlling style to get things done.	○	○	○	○	○
Avoids making difficult decisions; either requires more data than is needed, or seems reluctant to face tough issues.	○	○	○	○	○
Blames others for failures; does not take responsibility for mistakes.	○	○	○	○	○
Panics under pressure.	○	○	○	○	○
Demands results at all costs, regardless of the personal toll it may take on others.	○	○	○	○	○
Dismisses other colleagues and their ideas.	○	○	○	○	○
Is critical of others.	○	○	○	○	○
Escalates conflicts.	○	○	○	○	○
Gossips about colleagues behind their backs.	○	○	○	○	○
Makes negative and cynical comments.	○	○	○	○	○
Does not hold people accountable for results.	○	○	○	○	○
Does not keep promises.	○	○	○	○	○
Focuses on personal status, prestige, and ego, even if it hinders results.	○	○	○	○	○
Gets angry under pressure, which causes inappropriate behaviors.	○	○	○	○	○

Behavior	Frequency Of Each Behavior: Never	Rarely	Sometimes	Often	Always
Takes credit for the work of others.	○	○	○	○	○
Inflexible and rigid when making decisions.	○	○	○	○	○
Makes rash decisions and is too quick to act.	○	○	○	○	○
Does not listen to ideas and opinions.	○	○	○	○	○
Micro-manages rather than appropriately delegating responsibility and authority; seems unable to trust others to do the job.	○	○	○	○	○
Myopic about his or her own area of expertise; does not acknowledge the "big picture."	○	○	○	○	○
Fails to support staff and colleagues in developing their career paths.	○	○	○	○	○
Uses uncivil language and behavior.	○	○	○	○	○
Which of the above behaviors do you observe most often?					
Provide specific examples of times when he or she has shown these behaviors.					
What will it cost the person, and the organization, if these behaviors continue?					
What other behaviors, if any, would you suggest that he or she change?					
For each inappropriate behavior you have listed, describe a more productive behavior to use instead.					
What advice would you offer to help him or her change?					

For: ______________________

Your Name Here

The Survey No One Wants to Take (Abridged Version)

Are there any behaviors in particular that you would advise this person to change?

What's the most inappropriate behavior you have ever seen this person use at work? When?

Has he or she ever been arrogant, uncivil, self-righteous, or rigid? When?

When has this person avoided conflict, or avoided making tough decisions?

When have you observed his or her ego getting in the way?

What other behaviors, if any, should he or she change?

What are these behaviors costing this person, and the organization?

What advice would you offer this person to help modify these behaviors?

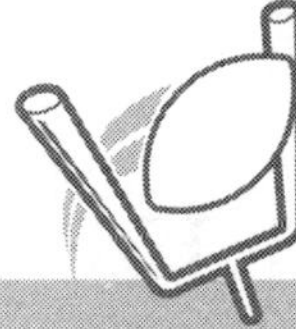

Set Goals for New Behavior

You now have information that will help you wipe your feet at the door. The next step is to set goals to change the behaviors that don't work.

Your goals should clearly state the behavior(s) you will change, how you will change, by when, and how you will measure the change.

Example:

"I will no longer dismiss other colleagues' ideas without carefully considering them. When someone presents a new idea, I will listen actively, ask questions, consider it thoughtfully, and thank the person for their idea. I may not accept the idea, but I will consider it. I will begin doing this immediately, and within six months, a survey will show that I have changed my behavior."

Use the following template to plan three goals you would like to reach. If you have trouble describing the new behavior(s), ask your colleagues for advice.

Worksheet: Setting Goals for Behavior Change

Old Behavior ("I will stop...")	New Behavior ("I will...")	Start Date	Date Behavior Is Changed	How I Will Measure This Change

Get Advice and Clear Up Past Mistakes

If you have completed *The Survey That No One Wants to Take* and have set goals to change your behavior, then you have shown a remarkable amount of courage. Few executives get this far. Ready for the next step? It takes as much courage and humility as the previous two.

The next step is to ask for advice and clear up past mistakes. Asking for advice from your colleagues accomplishes two objectives. First, it gives you the opportunity to get ideas from your colleagues. They are the ones who get to experience your behaviors—both effective and ineffective. They know how you can improve. Their advice could be invaluable to you and to your career.

Second, asking for advice strengthens professional relationships. Imagine going to a colleague, telling them about your goals to improve, and asking for advice. For instance, suppose that you said, "I've received a lot of feedback lately that I can be arrogant, and that this arrogance gets in my way. I'm trying to listen more, and dismiss others less. What advice would you give me about changing my behavior?" The simple act of admitting that you are trying to change for the better, and of involving others in your change, will make an immediate difference.

Asking for advice also offers an opportunity to clear up past mistakes. Because of our old behaviors, many of us have created a trail of resentment and weak professional relationships. This trail costs us a lot. If our relationships are weak, we can't expect others to perform at their best for us. We won't be able to make special requests for help and support. We can't expect others to trust our motivations and come to our aid in times of crisis. Morale, mutual respect with colleagues, and the willingness to collaborate and be part of a team suffer.

Clearing up past mistakes offers a way out of this situation. It can be painful for successful executives with large egos to do this, but it works.

For example, I recently coached the vice president of a large engineering firm who was furious at a colleague. During a project that the two co-managed, they fought constantly. While one left rude and angry voice mails, the other exploded during face-to-face conversations. The fight was costing them the respect of their staff and the client's satisfaction with the project.

Eventually, both agreed to have a meeting to discuss the issues between them. My client was prepared to go into that meeting fighting all the way, making accusations, and demanding that his colleague be more civil. I suggested that my client take responsibility for his own behavior in the situation, and start the meeting by clearing up his mistakes.

He took this advice. At the meeting, his colleague was shocked when my client began by saying, "I really want to apologize for my behavior. At least twice, I undermined your authority. I also apologize for hanging up on you last week. I had no right to do that, and it was disrespectful to you. Before we go on, is there anything else I did that contributed to this situation?" The colleague immediately softened, and they both focused on how to work together more productively in the future.

Again and again, I've seen how clearing up the past like this can repair, and even instantly restore, relationships. Clearing up past mistakes, along with asking for advice, also helps executives achieve some of their goals for changing behavior. Nothing helps a pushy, controlling executive become more collaborative and humble than asking for advice and clearing up past mistakes.

It takes three steps to clear up past mistakes:

Take responsibility for the mistake(s).

Give the other person a chance to vent.

Commit to changing your behavior going forward.

Admitting mistakes and clearing up the past doesn't mean that you have to yield on critical issues or give up your point of view. It only means that you are willing to change your behavior to be more effective.

This section continues on the next page. 

Now that you have data about the behaviors you want to change, get advice and clear up past mistakes. But before you do, think about whom you will speak to and what you will say. Let the worksheet below help you plan.

Worksheet: Get Advice / Clear Up Past Mistakes

Key Person I Will Approach For Advice	By When	The Advice I Will Ask For, and How I Will Ask	Past Mistakes I Am Prepared To Clear Up	What I Will Say To Make Amends

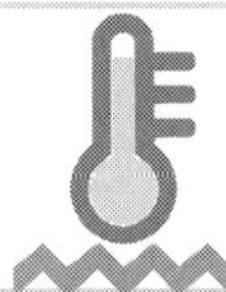

Measure Progress and Follow Up

The final step of wiping your feet at the door is to measure progress and follow up. Behaviors don't change overnight. Most likely, our unproductive behaviors have been cultivated over many years. They have become habits, and habits are hard to break. Even if we show initial improvement, we often retreat at the first sign of pressure or discomfort.

One effective way to measure progress is through a simple survey. In the example below, the executive has chosen to improve two behaviors: exercising civility and respect, and collaborating. The survey is designed so that participants can measure changes in behavior, from worse to better. By completing the survey every month (or at whatever interval you feel appropriate), you can get feedback about whether you are achieving your goals. A neutral party can help you conduct this survey so it is completely confidential.

Example: Survey to Measure Progress

Behavior	Progress, Compared With Month Before				
	Much Worse	Somewhat Worse	Same	Better	Much Better
Treated direct reports with civility and respect.	○	○	○	○	○
Collaborated with and listened to direct reports.	○	○	○	○	○

For areas that showed little or no improvement, please give specific examples.

What advice would you give this colleague about continuing to improve over the next month?

What other behaviors would you suggest that he or she stop, adopt, or change?

Now the process becomes foolproof! You become aware of behaviors you want to change through the latest survey results. Based on those results, you can set new goals, if appropriate. Next, you continue to ask for advice about how to improve, and clear up past mistakes. And finally, you measure progress and follow up again. When colleagues report that your behavior has become better or much better for two consecutive months, you can stop (or take *The Survey No One Wants to Take* again).

How will you measure progress and follow up? Use the worksheet below to plan.

Worksheet: Measuring Progress

Frequency Of Survey	People To Be Surveyed	Start Date

Take Care of Your Needs

Leadership demands discipline, focus, and energy. The job of leading can drain you. At the same time, if you don't take care of your personal needs, it is unlikely that you will be able to muster enough concentration and energy to inspire and mobilize others. By taking care of your needs—and even indulging in a few luxuries—you can recharge and rejuvenate.

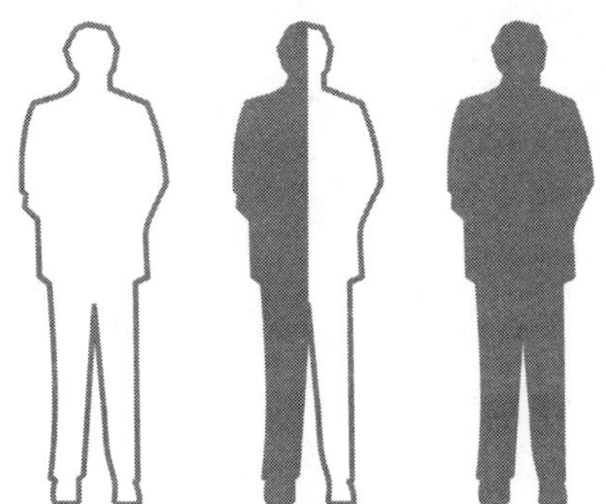

This chapter challenges you to put yourself first. Go ahead! What do you need to do to keep your edge? What can you do for yourself that will help you focus more clearly on achieving your goals? What can you do to better cope with daily crises and pressures? What can you do to rejuvenate yourself? What luxuries have you been putting off that will help you to recharge?

At the same time, what can you stop doing in order to focus better, and have more time and energy? What tasks can you delegate? What unhealthy habits can you stop?

Complete the following worksheet to begin thinking about how you can take care of your personal needs.

Worksheet: Take Care of Your Needs

Area Of Life	What Could You Do Or Have To Be More Focused, Have More Energy, And Recharge?	What Could You Stop Doing?
Health and nutrition		
Fitness		
Romance		
Family: children, spouse, parents, siblings, extended family		
The arts		

Area Of Life	What Could You Do Or Have To Be More Focused, Have More Energy, And Recharge?	What Could You Stop Doing?
Money and investments		
Knowledge		
Personal time		
Hobbies		
Friends		
Vacation and/or adventure		
Community and civic involvement		
Possessions/Luxuries		
Personal growth and development		
Spirituality		
Add your own: ________________		
Add your own: ________________		

Now, given the list you have completed, set some goals to take care of yourself.

Two needs I will take care of immediately:

	By when:
	By when:

Two needs I will take care of in the next two weeks:

	By when:
	By when:

One need I will take care of in the next month:

	By when:

One need I will take care of in the next quarter:

	By when:

Some leaders keep promises to others more faithfully than they keep promises to themselves. Consider asking a few colleagues, friends, and family members to support and help you keep these goals. By creating a support network, you increase the chances of truly taking care of your needs, and of staying recharged and rejuvenated as a leader.

Cultivate the Right Attitude

Leadership follows from the right attitude, and this chapter describes nine that enable elegant leadership. Leaders can cultivate any of these attitudes at any time to help improve satisfaction and performance at work:

Point a finger at yourself. In any situation—even those out of their immediate control—elegant leaders take responsibility for the results they get. They look at their own role in the situation, rather than blaming others or being a victim.

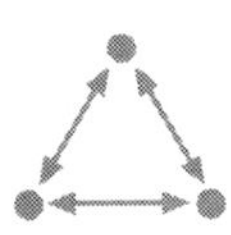

Balance ego, results, and relationships. Too much ego will lead an executive to focus more on looking good than on getting results and building relationships. At the same time, too much emphasis on either results or relationships can also impede effective leadership. Elegant leaders balance all three.

Embrace the "gray zone." A scuba diving term from New England, the "gray zone" is a metaphor for uncertainty, doubt, and ambiguity. Most leaders live in the gray zone during much of their work, and need to be comfortable there.

Learn from everything and everybody. After achieving success, some people let it go to their head. By assuming that they have learned it all, they stop taking advice, expanding their knowledge, or growing. Elegant leaders treat every situation as an opportunity to learn.

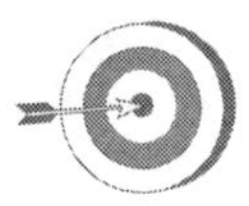

Become a master. Elegant leaders not only learn, they strive to become masters in their field. Masters achieve an exquisite level of performance, and have the patience and discipline to continue to improve.

Be a source of vision and opportunity. Elegant leaders see vision and opportunity when others don't.

Develop impeccable character. While others gradually compromise their principles and ethics, elegant leaders have exemplary character; they constantly question right and wrong, keep their word, and stand for what is right.

Be fulfilled—now. Fulfillment is a choice, and is not dependent on external circumstances or future events. Elegant leaders choose to be fulfilled, and become more effective as a result.

Be ready and willing to lead. Elegant leaders are ready and willing to lead whenever a situation calls for it—whether they feel like it or not.

Point a Finger at Yourself

In any situation, elegant leaders first point a finger at themselves. They take full responsibility for the quality of the results being produced, adjust their behavior to improve results, and continuously learn how to be more effective. They ask questions like:

Taking responsibility for situations goes way beyond taking blame. Blaming others is reactive, and connotes shame and guilt. Meanwhile, pointing a finger at one's self is proactive. It happens before, during, and after a situation. A leader who first points a finger at his or her self makes mid-course adjustments to get results, learns from mistakes, and continuously improves. This kind of leader even accepts responsibility for events out of his or her direct control, such as unanticipated market corrections, innovative moves by competitors, and changes in technology. Pointing a finger at one's self truly means: "The buck stops here."

Elegant leaders take responsibility while being smart about organizational politics. They don't announce to the press, or to the board, "I'm guilty; come and make me your scapegoat." But people can count on them to own up to their role in a situation in an appropriate way, and take proactive steps to improve results.

When do you take responsibility, and how could you improve? Take the assessment on the following page to find out (and ask colleagues to validate your answers).

Self-Assessment: Taking Responsibility

	No	Yes
If I don't have the intended impact when communicating with someone, I try another approach rather than assuming that the other person is flawed.	○	○
When business results are poor, I first look at my own role in the situation, and admit my mistakes.	○	○
When my professional relationship with another person is weak, I ask how I have contributed to the situation before blaming the other person.	○	○
In times of conflict, I take responsibility for my actions before asking the other person to take responsibility for his or her actions.	○	○
When market conditions change and the organization suffers, I take responsibility for not anticipating the change—even though the direction of the market is beyond my immediate control.	○	○
Under pressure, I resist the urge to attack or blame others.	○	○
Under pressure, I carefully consider the appropriate response. I do not react according to my impulses and feelings.	○	○
When others take responsibility by admitting their mistakes, I put the past in the past rather than hold grudges. I thank the person for taking responsibility and work with him or her to move forward.	○	○

What, if any, insights did you gain about improving your performance by first pointing a finger at yourself?

Balance Ego, Results, and Relationships

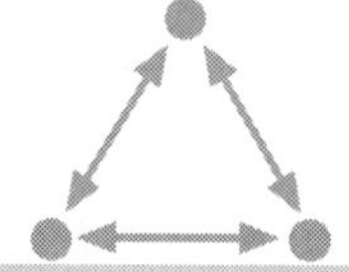

Leaders successfully balance three tensions: satisfying their ego, achieving results, and building powerful relationships. This section explores the connections among all three.

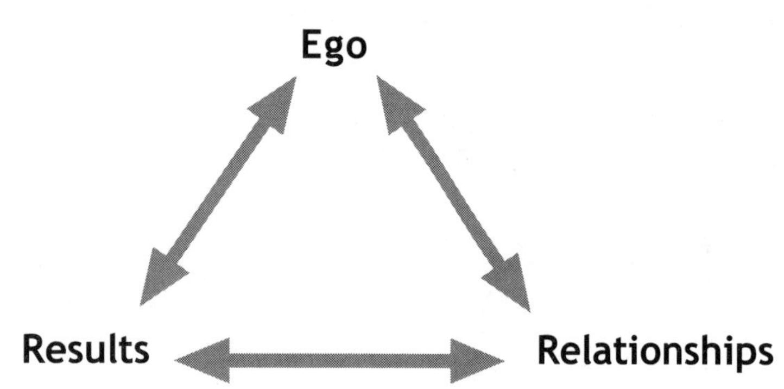

Ego. Ego represents our sense of self, and the gratification we get from success, power, status, prestige, and simply looking good in front of others. Many Eastern philosophies and management gurus assume that ego is 100 percent bad, not to mention illusory. This book takes a more balanced view. On the one hand, a strong ego can give leaders the confidence to persist in the face of setbacks, to set audacious goals, and to raise the bar. Whether illusory or real, a strong sense of self helps to drive results.

On the other hand, a strong ego can also get in the way. With too much ego, leaders sacrifice results and relationships for status, power, prestige, and credit. For instance, I worked with a healthcare organization that was deep in the red. The executive team wisely set up a process to involve all employees in developing ideas to reduce costs while maintaining the quality of patient care. Unfortunately, as the process began, it became clear that these executives wanted to see cuts made at the bottom of the organization before they made any cuts at their level. At least 20 employees anonymously submitted the idea that the CEO and other top managers should cancel their corporate country club memberships, which were costing the organization $50,000 annually. Each of the top managers balked at the idea; they also refused to cut their car allowance or reduce the number of their administrative assistants. Ultimately, the organization failed to achieve its goals, and the employees became increasingly cynical and resentful. The executives' focus on ego over results and relationships certainly contributed to this outcome.

Ironically, the best way to satisfy one's ego is by first focusing on building strong relationships and getting results. With results and relationships in place, status, power, prestige and credit almost always follow.

There are many signs of too much ego. The following self-assessment presents a few ways to tell whether you put too much emphasis on gratifying your own ego. If you check "no" to any of these comments, then your ego might be getting in the way.

Self-Assessment: Does Your Ego Get in the Way?

	No	Yes
I constantly find ways to give credit where it's due.	○	○
	○	○
To me, leadership is situational. When it's time to move on, I get out of the way and let others take over. I can give at least three examples of when I have done this.	○	○
	○	○
I take risks even if I might look foolish in front of other people.	○	○
	○	○
I understand that I cannot control everything. Sometimes I need to trust and rely on other people to get results. Other times, I need to surrender to the process, and have faith that things will work out. If asked, my colleagues would say that I trust others, and am willing to give up control, without abdicating responsibility.	○	○
	○	○
I make decisions based first on getting results and strengthening relationships. I believe that personal gain will follow naturally if results and relationships are in place.	○	○
	○	○
I do not claim to have all the answers and welcome ideas from other people. I do not dismiss ideas from others without considering them carefully.	○	○

Results. Leaders live and die by the results they get. And they get these results by knowing how to set goals, move things forward, build momentum, get resources, hold people accountable, and achieve specific outcomes.

However, an overemphasis on results, without maintaining relationships, will not last. Employees and colleagues will feel coerced, or forced. They will comply with your demands, but resent you. Eventually, they will respond to your orders and formal authority, but not develop respect or regard for you. They may go along with what you want, but not commit to you or your vision. In a crisis, your people may not make the personal sacrifices required to pull through.

The following self-assessment presents a few ways to tell whether you put too much emphasis on results. If you check "no" to any of these comments, then you might be forcing or coercing others to get what you want.

Self-Assessment: Do You Overemphasize Results?

	No	Yes
In every situation with a colleague, I ask two questions: "Am I getting results?" and, "Am I preserving and building the relationship in a way that is appropriate for this situation?"	○	○
When employees and colleagues do not meet my expectations, I apply pressure. However, I make sure that the pressure I apply matches the situation. For instance, when somebody makes a relatively minor mistake, I don't automatically put him or her on probation.	○	○
I want results, but will not yell or use abusive language to get them.	○	○
After a project ends, the people who were on my team still want to maintain a relationship with me. In fact, many former teammates request to work with me again.	○	○
I do not have a reputation as a "churn and burn" leader. Voluntary attrition on my team is lower than in the rest of the organization.	○	○
It is unlikely that my colleagues and direct reports would give me a nickname like "Rambo," "drill sergeant," or "pit bull."	○	○
When I work with other people on projects, I try my best to help them succeed, both personally and professionally.	○	○
It takes a lot for me to "write somebody off." When people make mistakes, I use their mistakes as an opportunity for everybody to learn.	○	○

Relationships. To succeed, leaders need to develop strong professional relationships with key people who will help them achieve remarkable results. Leaders build relationships as part of a conscious strategy. They invest time and energy in both the business and personal aspects of the relationship. To strengthen relationships, leaders see the potential in other people, forgive past mistakes, get over petty resentments, admit their own mistakes, and acknowledge others for their contributions.

However, as with ego and results, overemphasizing relationships can cause problems. People who focus too much on relationships might not get anything done. They become too concerned with being popular and with avoiding conflict. They fail to make tough decisions, and seem to prefer harmony and peace to open and honest dialogue.

Ironically, those who focus too much on relationships eventually develop weak relationships because they fail to insist on high standards and getting results. Their relationships become inauthentic, based on popularity rather than on substance.

Do you overemphasize relationships? Take the following self-assessment. If you check "no" to any of these answers, think about ways to better balance relationships with results and ego.

Self-Assessment: Do You Overemphasize Relationships?

	No	Yes
When a situation gets tense, I assert my needs appropriately. I do not avoid conflict to protect the relationship.	○	○
When somebody is not meeting my expectations, I tell the person directly what I want him or her to do differently. I do not hold back tough feedback to protect the relationship.	○	○
I am comfortable when people express differences during meetings, even if it leads to conflict. I do not try to mediate and bring harmony to avoid productive discussions.	○	○
I understand the difference between being respected and being popular, and prefer being respected.	○	○
I regularly assess the performance of my team, and remove mediocre performers, regardless of whether I like them personally or not.	○	○
I spend time thinking about how to strengthen relationships with key people, while still getting results.	○	○

Are you in balance? Most of us tend to lean toward one or two of the three sides of the ego, results, and relationships triangle. Under pressure, when the famous "fight or flight" reaction emerges, we especially lean to one side or the other. People who tend to fight under pressure focus on results and/or ego. Those who tend to flee under pressure focus on avoiding conflict and preserving relationships.

By becoming conscious of our natural bias toward ego, relationships, or results, we can choose an optimal balance. That way, we will get results, while also strengthening relationships and, in the end, satisfying our own sense of self.

The last two questions of this section will help you balance ego, results, and relationships more effectively:

Under pressure, I tend to overemphasize (check up to two of the following):

○ Ego ○ Results ○ Relationships

Following are up to three things I can do differently—especially when under pressure—to bring ego, results, and relationships into balance for me:

1

2

3

Embrace the Gray Zone

Scuba divers in the cold and murky waters of New England occasionally confront what they call the "gray zone." Imagine that you are in full scuba gear and jump from a dive boat off the Cape Cod coast. You plan to descend to the ocean floor, 65 feet below. At about 30 feet, you notice that, when you look up toward the surface of the water, you see nothing—except for the boat's anchor line disappearing into grayness. When you look down, you see nothing again, except for the anchor line disappearing into the grayness below. All around you, you see nothing but gray. Welcome to the gray zone.

Many novice divers do not like this place. But, those who continue their descent calmly through the gray zone almost always cherish the experience. While eerie, the gray zone itself can be a remarkable place, a peaceful place where one floats in nothingness. Even better, after descending for a few minutes the ocean floor gradually comes into focus. Perhaps you see the hull of an historic shipwreck, or a huge lobster sitting on the ocean floor. Diving into the gray zone is almost always worth it.

Leading organizations is a lot like diving through the gray zone. It's not for everyone, and it's sometimes scary. However, those who persist and cope—even in the face of risk, uncertainty, and ambiguity—almost always reap rewards.

Leaders who embrace the gray zone tolerate, and even thrive on uncertainty. They experiment and try new things, and invite others to explore the unknown with them. They learn from failure, stay calm under pressure, and bounce back when things don't quite work out.

One of the essential attitudes of elegant leadership is the ability to embrace uncertainty and ambiguity—to swim in the gray zone. How do you perform in the gray zone? Answer the questions on the following page to get a better idea.

Turn to the self-assessment on the next page.

Self-Assessment: How Do You Face Uncertainty?

How do you react in times of uncertainty and ambiguity? (Check one.)

- ○ I panic and overreact.
- ○ I rush to an answer and to action. I prefer acting rapidly on my own than exploring with others.
- ○ I resist uncertainty. I change only when absolutely necessary, and sometimes when it is too late.
- ○ I embrace uncertainty. I enjoy the process of exploring new territory while forging ahead. I encourage and challenge my colleagues to explore with me.
- ○ I may be too much of an adventurer. I tend to put the organization at risk by experimenting and exploring, even when it is not necessary.

How did your parents react in the face of uncertainty? What did they teach you about taking risks and dealing with the unknown? How does this reflect your beliefs about taking risks and embracing uncertainty?

Who is the most resilient, unflappable person that you know? What can you learn from this person about entering the unknown, taking risks, coping, and bouncing back from mistakes?

What's the biggest risk you ever took? What did you learn about risk by taking it?

What has been the point of greatest uncertainty in your organization? In your career? How did you respond? Who did you involve? How did you involve them? What would you do differently next time?

Learn from Everything and Everybody

After experiencing so much success, some leaders conclude that they know it all. They stop asking for advice and feedback. They dismiss others' ideas. They scorn those who offer constructive feedback.

This arrogance can get leaders into big trouble, and fast. Without a way to continue to learn and develop, anybody—including the founders of successful companies—can fall into a rut. If the environment changes, and the leader does not, both the leader and the organization can suffer.

One way to avoid this type of failure is by being open to advice, feedback, and support. Effective leaders consider ideas from a wide range of sources, including colleagues, board members, staff, and outsiders. They actively seek advice about how they can improve their own performance and behaviors and surround themselves with smart people who can challenge their thinking. They develop support networks so that they can call on trusted colleagues about a range of issues.

Leaders also learn from key experiences. They seek to understand how to replicate success, and to get better after failures. They learn from colleagues during and after projects, and constantly work to discover how things can be better.

This openness to learning is an attitude, a way of being. Effective leaders welcome the opportunity to learn more, to explore things they don't know, and enter into territory they never even knew existed.

How open are you to continuous learning, advice, and feedback? Take the following assessment to find out. What can you do better?

Turn to the self-assessment on the next page. 

Self-Assessment: How Open Are You to Continuous Learning?

	No	Yes
I take advice and support from others, but only when I am in pain and really need it.	○	○
I request, and consider, advice from my direct reports. When they give me tough feedback, I listen to it and thank them, without getting defensive.	○	○
I frequently request advice and feedback from my manager. When he or she gives me tough feedback, I listen to it and thank him or her, without getting defensive.	○	○
I frequently seek advice and feedback from my top customers. When they give me tough feedback, I listen to it and thank them, without getting defensive.	○	○
I frequently seek advice from my colleagues. When they give me tough feedback, I listen to it and thank them, without getting defensive.	○	○
I graciously accept advice and feedback from anybody who offers it, even if I don't ask for it. When someone gives me tough feedback, I listen to it and thank him or her, without getting defensive.	○	○
When I get tough feedback that is accurate, I readily admit my mistakes and take action to improve.	○	○
I create an atmosphere where people feel comfortable approaching me to give me advice, even difficult advice.	○	○
I have built up a network of people who can challenge my thinking and provide emotional support when I need it.	○	○
I frequently invest in professional development, from learning more about my industry to becoming a more effective leader.	○	○
I treat every situation and every interaction as an opportunity to learn and improve. My manager, direct reports, and colleagues would agree.	○	○
I surround myself with people who are smarter than I am.	○	○

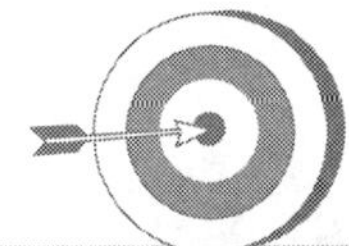

Become a Master

Leaders not only learn from everyone and everything, they also strive to become masters. Becoming a master means continuously improving in your area of expertise until you are the best in the world, until you intuitively know how to perform exquisitely.

Mastery takes time, patience, practice, and discipline. Few people become masters. Some prefer to experiment with many different activities and pursuits. Others try, but give up along the way when they hit their first roadblock or failure. Others give up when they have trouble reaching the next level of performance, and consequently get bored.

Mastery is less an end point than a process and an attitude. People striving for mastery practice their skills religiously. They persist when they encounter obstacles, or long plateaus without improvement. They develop a mindset that combines discipline, focus, curiosity, passion, and persistence.

This section challenges you to openly declare an area, or areas, that you will master during your career. (For more information, George Leonard's book *Mastery* is an excellent resource.)

Answer the questions that follow:

Given the strategic challenges your organization faces, and given where the industry is headed, what are the crucial areas of expertise that you must possess to be the best? List key areas of knowledge, contacts, achievements, functional expertise, experiences, and skills.

For each of the areas that you mentioned, what can you do in the next few months to become better? (*For example: get a coach, meet with a mentor, meet key people in the industry, join a networking group or industry association, begin a formal training program, request a new assignment, get a new customer, and/or study on your own.*)

Knowing what you know about yourself, what situations might arise to cause you to give up your path to mastery? How will you keep going when you face these situations?

Based on your work above, formally declare your area of mastery:

Examples: *"I will know more about the paper industry than anybody else in the world." — Paper industry analyst*

"I will know more about mergers and acquisitions law than any other lawyer." — Associate at a prominent law firm

Be a Source of Vision and Opportunity

Leaders have vision. They see endless possibilities to create a more compelling, inspiring future. They work with others to create a shared vision that involves, inspires, and motivates as many people as possible. When people get lost in daily tasks and crises, leaders remind them about what will be possible, thanks to their hard work. When people express doubt, leaders build resolve by reminding them of the group's shared vision.

At the same time, leaders create opportunities to take action and move toward the vision. They shift comfortably from talking about a general vision to identifying specific opportunities to pursue. Meanwhile, when people begin to complain about a situation, but do nothing to fix it, leaders find solutions. When most people accept the status quo, leaders seek out and find ways to do things better. When progress on a crucial project halts (or takes a step backwards) and people want to give up, leaders identify opportunities to move forward. Even in the most difficult situations, they assume there is a way to succeed and make things better. In fact, when other people complain or become negative, a leader's resolve to improve the situation only increases.

Do you work hard to create an inspiring vision that includes as many people as possible? Do you see opportunity everywhere and always, or do you sit back, complain, and give up when things get tough? This section will help you find out. It does that first by focusing on vision, then on opportunity.

First, are you a source of vision? This section assesses your ability to develop vision. The worksheet below lists a number of areas that leaders encounter at work. For each area, describe your vision. Remember to paint an inspiring, compelling picture—one that will excite others. You may want to recall the vision you created in Chapter One.

After you are done, ask colleagues to rate your vision on a scale of one to five (1 = Boring; 2 = Neutral; 3 = Lukewarm; 4 = Getting there; 5 = Compelling and inspiring). Then, have them complete the survey that follows.

Worksheet: Identify Vision

Area	My Vision In Three To Five Years	Colleagues' Ratings (1 to 5)
My organization		
Our quality and service		
My career and job		

Area	My Vision In Three To Five Years	Colleagues' Ratings (1 to 5)
The members of my team (their career and job)		
My manager's career and job		
Our customers, thanks to our products and services		
The culture in my organization		
Any or all of the following functions: information technology, human resources, finance, marketing, sales, product development, business development, and R&D		
New products and services		
Current projects and initiatives		
Any other areas:		

Now, ask your colleagues to complete the following assessment to evaluate how visionary you are:

For: ______________________________
Your Name Here

Assessment: How Visionary Are You?

	Strongly Disagree	Disagree	Neutral	Agree	Strongly Agree
He or she frequently involves others in developing a compelling, shared vision of what is possible.	○	○	○	○	○
When others are doubtful and skeptical, he or she remains positive and optimistic.	○	○	○	○	○
He or she renews others' flagging energy and commitment by sharing an inspiring and compelling vision about the future.	○	○	○	○	○
I would say that this person is a visionary, able to identify future trends and possibilities that few others see.	○	○	○	○	○
He or she speaks frequently about how the future will be better, thanks to our work together.	○	○	○	○	○
He or she uses colorful, active, interesting language to paint a picture of the future that people can actually imagine and feel.	○	○	○	○	○
He or she expresses vision in terms that matter to others, not just in terms that will make his or her own life better.	○	○	○	○	○
He or she successfully balances a focus on current deadlines and tasks with a view toward future direction and possibilities.	○	○	○	○	○

Based on your work above, how would you assess your capacity for vision? What are your areas for improvement? What advice or insights did your colleagues provide?

Are you a source of opportunities? As suggested earlier, opportunities are specific initiatives and projects that solve problems, make things better, and help people move toward their vision.

The following worksheet challenges you to identify as many opportunities as you can. It lists a variety of areas that most leaders experience in their work. It includes everything from specific functional areas you might work with to specific people. For each area, list any complaints, grudges, problems, resentments, or concerns that you have. At the same time, list opportunities for improvement in each area. These opportunities might resolve any issues you have listed, or simply be ways to improve the status quo.

Opportunities should be initiatives or conversations that you can have to make things better. For instance, suppose that one of your issues is that the shipping department does not respond quickly enough to rush orders. An opportunity might be to work with the head of the department to develop a custom process to handle rush orders in a way that is profitable for the company.

After you finish, complete the survey that follows the worksheet.

Worksheet: Identify Issues and Opportunities

Area	Issues, Problems, Complaints, Resentments, Concerns	Opportunities
Alignment among the executive team		
Key customers (list):		
Products and services that we offer (list):		
Key projects and initiatives underway (list):		
My career (e.g., my authority, compensation, position, and voice in the company)		
Key competitors (list):		
Strategic partners (list):		
Culture and environment in the company		
Key functions: information technology, human resources, finance, marketing, sales, product development, business development, and R&D		
Key colleagues: direct reports, boss, peers, investors, and board members		
Any other areas:		

Given your answers on the previous page, complete the following:

Calculate the following:

How many opportunities did you identify—even though you had no specific problem or issue for that area?

Count the number of opportunities you identified, then the number of issues you raised. What is the ratio of opportunities to issues?

For what percentage of your issues have you already identified an opportunity and taken action?

For what percentage of issues have you identified an opportunity but not taken action?

For what percentage of your issues have you identified no opportunity?

Are you satisfied with the above ratios? Do you believe that the balance you have struck between problems and opportunities is acceptable? Where might you have room to improve?

For each of your issues in which you have not acted, will you continue being concerned, let the issue go, or take action? What does your answer reveal about your capacity to identify and follow through with opportunities?

Given this exercise, how would you assess your capacity for seeking out opportunity everywhere, all the time? How would you assess your persistence in resolving issues to a satisfactory conclusion?

Develop Impeccable Character

People with impeccable character keep their promises, proactively explore right and wrong, involve key stakeholders in critical decisions that will affect lives, and take a stand when people in the organization act with questionable morals.

Character is critical, and it rests on a slippery slope. Most of us make little decisions every day that determine the quality of our character. Some of us have already compromised our character with seemingly minor issues, rationalizing them as trivial. Perhaps we mislead employees about their prospects with the company, avoid speaking honestly about our motivations, or say we support decisions while covertly resisting them. Or, perhaps we put a spin on press releases that is not entirely accurate, or allocate a shipment to the wrong quarter in order to make our goal. From there, it is a relatively short leap to compromising more frequently, or on even more serious issues. It becomes comfortable to rationalize our actions in the name of the free market, investor demands, competitive pressures, or the goal of being number one. Eventually, an entire organization can create systematic ways to avoid doing what is right.

This section challenges you to assess your own character and correct past mistakes. In the worksheet that follows, grade yourself (or have somebody else grade you) on your overall character. Then give specific examples to support your grade.

Worksheet: Assessing Character

	My Grade (A, B, C, D)	Examples of How I Have Shown Character
Being truthful with, and keeping my word to employees, customers, investors, my manager, and colleagues.		
Putting the values of the organization into action.		
Having open and honest conversations with everyone I meet.		
Keeping my commitments (e.g., attending and being on time to meetings, providing promised resources, and meeting deadlines).		
Ensuring that financial statements are accurate and do not mislead investors or the government.		

Continued

Worksheet: Assessing Character

	My Grade (A, B, C, D)	Examples Of How I Have Shown Character
Ensuring that employees are safe in their working environment.		
Ensuring that products are safe, and acting immediately if they are not.		
Presenting the organization accurately to the public.		
Ensuring that we have a diverse workforce at all levels of the organization.		
Ensuring that all employees and customers are treated fairly.		
Ensuring that employees and customers are treated with dignity, respect, and civility.		
Keeping promises made to customers.		
Being honest during the recruiting process about expectations and roles.		
Respecting and being a steward of our environment.		
Supporting the communities where we work.		
Asking ethical questions when the organization makes key decisions.		
Periodically assessing the organization's ethics and character.		
Other areas:		

How did you rate yourself? Based on the worksheet, answer the following questions:

In what areas did you not get an "A" grade? How far down the slippery slope have you fallen? Are you willing to make amends for these areas?

For each area in which you did not get an "A," what can you start doing differently now? What questions can you ask? What requests can you make? What stand can you take?

What else can you do to develop impeccable character?

How would you rate your organization based on these same questions? What can you do about areas where your organization falls short?

Be Fulfilled—Now

Most people assume that fulfillment comes later. They assume that if only they had something that they don't have now, they would be completely and totally satisfied. Their "if only's" include more money, a college degree, an initial public offering, a buyer for the company, more time, a trip around the world, and many others. Of course, as soon as they get or do what they thought would lead to fulfillment, they find another "if only." In our culture, mass media supplies an endless list of "if only's" that supposedly help people become fulfilled.

Meanwhile, elegant leaders recognize that fulfillment is a choice we can make right now. There is no reason to wait to be fulfilled. We can be satisfied, at peace, and joyful in the present moment. Fulfillment is an attitude, a way of experiencing life. It has nothing to do with our circumstances, or what we intend to do in the future.

This definition of fulfillment is a hard sell. Lots of people seem to think that fulfillment requires certain external conditions; that we have to earn the right to be fulfilled. They resist the idea that right now, in this very moment, any of us—especially executives—can choose to be fulfilled.

Leaders who choose fulfillment have an advantage over those who don't. They are calmer in the face of crisis, more objective, resilient in the face of setbacks, and a continual source of resolve and confidence. While others panic, fulfilled leaders have perspective—a perspective grounded in the context of the gift of life itself. People are naturally attracted to leaders who are fulfilled because these same leaders are also fully alive, and engaged and passionate about what they do.

People who choose to be fulfilled make 10 assumptions:

1. Fulfillment is a choice.
2. The universe constantly changes and we can resist this change or embrace it.
3. It is fine to strive for goals, and if things don't go our way, we can accept the results, learn from them, and move forward.
4. It is important to enjoy the present moment, plan for the future, and learn from the past.
5. We humans need to lighten up.
6. Express gratitude daily for all that we have.
7. Take responsibility for our attitude, experience, and feelings.
8. It can always be worse.
9. We can choose to be fulfilled even when we think we aren't.
10. Being fulfilled takes awareness and practice.

What would it take for you to be fulfilled right now? Answer these questions:

What beliefs do you have about fulfillment and work? Which of these beliefs make it difficult for you to accept that fulfillment can happen right now?

What would it take for you to decide that your team is staffed with brilliant superstars? What would it take for you to feel honored and privileged to be allowed to work with them?

What would it take to make your next meeting (that you are dreading) the greatest and most productive meeting possible?

What would it take to make your current assignment the most extraordinary and rewarding career experience you have ever had?

What would it take to make this quarter the most fascinating and rewarding quarter yet? What could you do right now to make that happen?

How can you lighten up—either about work or about yourself—to be more fulfilled? How can you be easier on yourself?

Continued 

What attributes could you develop that would help you be more fulfilled? Check two or three of those listed below, and consider ways to bring them into your professional and personal life.

- ○ Improvisation
- ○ Gratitude
- ○ Passion
- ○ Adventure
- ○ Curiosity
- ○ Spirituality
- ○ Relaxation
- ○ Serenity
- ○ Peace
- ○ Trust
- ○ Optimism
- ○ Forgiveness
- ○ Joy
- ○ Spontaneity
- ○ Creativity
- ○ Humor
- ○ Playfulness

The above questions are challenging. Some people respond cynically to them: "The way to make the next meeting fulfilling is by canceling it." Others fall back into the "if only" mode: "Increase our marketing budget and things will be fine." Finally, some executives insist that these questions are immature and naïve: "Work is not fun; that's why they pay us." If you fit into one of these categories, have it your way. For some people, it takes a lifetime to understand that fulfillment can happen in the blink of an eye.

For the rest of you, please ponder this riddle: What would it take for you to be totally and completely fulfilled right now?

Be Ready and Willing to Lead

Finally, elegant leaders are always ready and willing to lead. They don't always need to step in and lead, and sometimes they get out of the way and let others do the leading, but they are always ready and willing. They constantly ask, "How can I serve?" To use a metaphor from physics, they are a "potential field" of leadership.

Being willing to lead means leading even when you don't feel like it. It means focusing on results and what the situation needs, instead of focusing on you. As the matrix below shows, people fall into four categories, based on their feelings and their actions:

The walking dead. These people never feel like leading.

Procrastinators and whiners. These people feel like leading, but never take action. They have to live with the disappointment of having high aspirations but little or no follow-up.

The lucky few. These people feel like leading, and take action to lead. Most leaders fall into this category some of the time, but not always.

Elegant leaders. Elegant leaders lead even when they don't want to. They overcome their desire to complain or quit, and do what it takes to achieve their vision and mission.

The Elegant Leadership Matrix

	Doesn't Feel Like Leading	Feels Like Leading
Takes Action And Leads	**Elegant leaders**	**The lucky few**
Takes No Action	**The walking dead**	**Procrastinators and whiners**

Think about the most challenging situations you and your organization face right now. Then, answer the following questions about your readiness and willingness to lead:

1 For each situation, where would you place yourself on the above matrix?

2 How often do you find yourself not feeling like leading? In what types of situations? How do you manage to take action despite the way you feel?

3 What advice would you give to others about being ready and willing to lead, even when they don't feel like it?

Develop an Elegant Strategy

Thanks to an oversupply of management consultants and scholars, strategy has become too complex. Jargon in books and business journals creates the impression that only specialized experts have the brainpower to create a strategy. Meanwhile, many executives entrust their thinking to management consultants, who in turn charge exorbitant fees for brilliant documents that nobody uses.

In fact, strategy can be simple, practical, powerful, and graceful. More importantly, people inside a company have all the knowledge they need to develop an elegant strategy on their own. This chapter shows you how.

Put simply, a strategy defines how an organization will excel in the marketplace. A strategy answers the following questions:

- What should your organization do best?
- Against which competitors?
- With which products and services?
- For which customers?
- What tactics will help you beat the competition?

This chapter describes 10 simple steps for developing an elegant strategy:

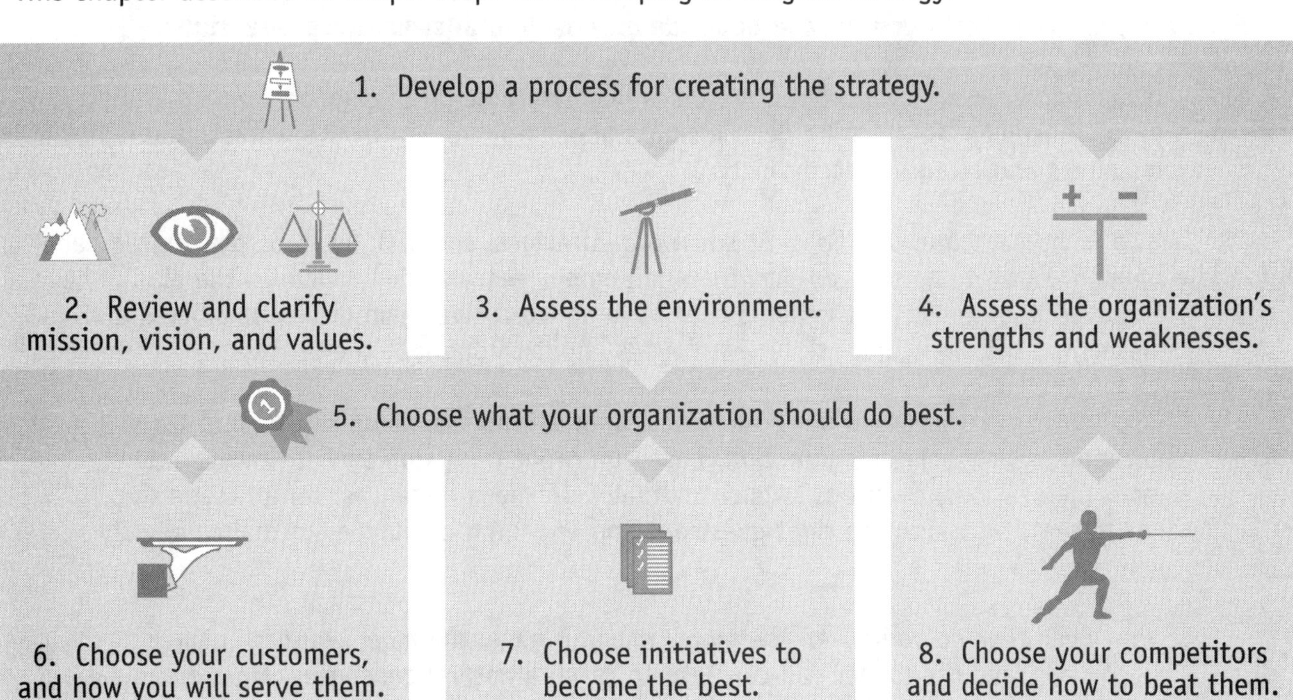

9. Develop messages for the market.

10. Synthesize and clearly communicate the strategy.

Develop a Process for Creating the Strategy

Developing a strategy requires an effective process that follows four guidelines:

1. ***Trust the organization.*** An effective process does not rely on external, self-proclaimed experts for the answers. Instead, it trusts that the organization's own people know enough to develop an elegant strategy.

2. ***Involve the people who know.*** An effective process involves employees closest to the customer, competition, and products, because these people have firsthand knowledge of the marketplace.

3. ***Share and synthesize information.*** An effective process breaks down barriers among different business units, functions, and processes. It brings together knowledge from up, down, and across the organization.

4. ***Get results.*** An effective process gets results. While it may take some time to develop and execute a strategy, ultimately it should lead to an improved position in the marketplace, and better financial performance.

Beyond those guidelines, there are many possible ways to develop a strategy in your organization. **The process you choose depends on how you answer these questions:**

What is the outcome you want? Outcomes of a strategic process range from creating a formal document to reaching deep insights about how to win in the market, and shifting resources and attention accordingly.

Who will participate, and how? At some organizations, the CEO develops the strategy and hands it down to employees. At others, all employees provide input into the plan. I have achieved good results with clients that have an executive team drive the process and make final decisions, but ask for employees' input throughout the process.

Who makes decisions, and how? At most organizations, the senior leadership team determines final strategic direction, based on input from employees. However, at a few organizations, decisions happen naturally. In these instances, senior leadership trusts that, by asking the right questions and engaging employees in dialogue, answers will emerge.

How much time do you have? The more time you have, the more you can involve employees, and the longer you can take to reach a natural consensus. Most organizations can develop a strategy in three to six months, assuming that the leadership team meets regularly to discuss results and make decisions.

With these questions in mind, most executives appreciate a process with clearly defined meetings, decisions, and end dates. An illustrative schedule for such a process follows. Different organizations adjust the schedule accordingly, for instance to budget more or less time to involve employees, to increase or decrease the number of meetings, or to meet a deadline.

Illustrative Schedule for Formal Strategy Development Process

Step	Timing
Ask employees to collect data about market and competitive trends, as well as the organization's strengths and weaknesses. Also review and clarify the organization's mission, vision, and values.	One month
Retreat One: Review and, if necessary, rewrite, the organization's mission, vision, and values. Synthesize key market and competitive trends, as well as the organization's strengths and weaknesses. The retreat ends by beginning to consider what the organization does, and should do best.	One to two days
Share results of Retreat One with employees, and get their input about what the organization does, and should do, best.	One month
Retreat Two: Determine how the organization will focus its resources and attention. Specifically, what should the organization do best? For which customers, and with which products?	One to two days
Share results of Retreat Two with employees, and get their input about initiatives to support the decisions made during that retreat.	One month
Retreat Three: Develop initiatives to support the strategic focus. Define competitors, tactics to beat competitors, and key messages to the market. Synthesize the final strategy into a concise document.	One to two days
Share results of Retreat Three with employees. Have each department develop a plan to support the strategy. Begin planning and budgeting process as appropriate.	One month, and ongoing
Repeat the process annually or bi-annually.	

Given the information presented about process, answer the following questions to plan your process for developing a strategy:

What is the outcome you want from the process?

Who will lead the process?

Who will be involved from senior leadership? What will be their roles?

Which other employees will be involved? How will they provide input? Which employees will not be involved?

How will decisions be made?

By when does the process need to be complete?

Who will develop the schedule, participant lists, and agenda? Who will drive the process of involving employees and synthesizing their input?

How would you adapt the sample schedule provided in this section to meet your organization's needs?

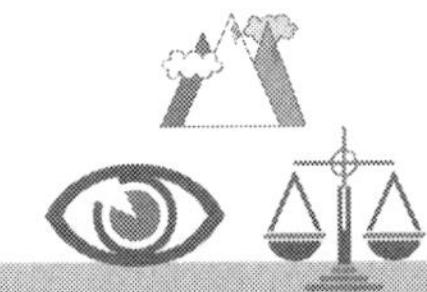

Mission, Vision, and Values

Strategy depends in part on an organization's mission, vision, and values. The mission describes the organization's aspirations and reason(s) for existing. Strategy sets the path to help achieve those aspirations, no matter how idealistic they may seem. Vision paints a picture of what the organization will become in the future. An elegant strategy helps it get there. Finally, values describe the standards and principles employees will use to work together now and in the future. Values set the tone for how the strategy will be developed and implemented.

Chapter One of this book already challenged you to express your mission, vision, and values for your organization and work. While that may ground you on an individual level, employees throughout the organization should agree on the company's mission, vision and values.

Fill in the spaces below so you will have this information handy as you develop your strategy.

Your organization's mission:

Your organization's vision:

Your organization's values:

Assess the Environment

Creating a strategy can't happen in a vacuum. A large part of developing a strategy involves understanding the external environment, including customers, competitors, new technology, government, and the labor market. A proper assessment should look at the environment today, and scenarios for how the environment might evolve in the future. This section asks you some essential questions for assessing your external environment.

Understand your customers. First, understand your customers by answering the following questions:

Who are your customers today?

How do you divide your customers into segments (e.g., by geography, age, income, size or type of purchases, lifestyle)?

Which segments will be more important over the next few years? Less important? Why?

Which segments have been most profitable for your organization? Which segments have been least profitable? Why?

Which segments are currently not customers, but could or should be?

For each segment that you identified as important—either today or in the future—fill in the following worksheet.

Worksheet: Assessing Customer Segments

Name of Segment: ____________________

	Today	In Three To Five Years
Description of this segment:		
How big is this segment in terms of volume and revenue?		

	Today	In Three To Five Years
What is your organization's market share in this segment?		
What are the key requirements and buying criteria for this segment?		
How does this segment become aware of a need for your products and services? How do they decide to make a purchase?		
What does this segment perceive to be substitutes for your products and/or services?		
Who competes with your organization for this segment's loyalty?		
What opportunities exist to better serve this segment?		
How profitable is this segment for your organization?		
How strong a fit is this segment with your organization's current strategy, including your products and services?		

What are the implications of this information on your organization's strategy?

Assess the competition. Next, assess your competitors by first answering the following three questions. Then, for each competitor, complete the competitive assessment that follows.

Who are your major competitors?

Who might enter the market and become a competitor?

What substitutes for your products and services represent potential competition? (For instance, public transport is a potential substitute for taxis.)

For each competitor, potential entrant, or substitute, complete the following worksheet.

Worksheet: Competitor Assessment

Competitor Name: ______________________

On what basis does this competitor compete?	
In which customer segments, or with which products, does this competitor lead the market? Why?	
What are this competitor's strengths?	
What are this competitor's weaknesses?	
How does the competitor compare to your organization—in terms of cost, quality, service, speed, and technology?	
What could this competitor do to take customers away from your organization?	
What strategic alliances could this competitor build to hurt your position in the market?	
What could this competitor do to make customers more loyal to them?	

How could this competitor develop significant scale, in a way that makes their products more attractive?	
What could this competitor do to gain greater power over suppliers than your organization commands?	
How could this competitor use technology to gain a significant advantage?	
How could this competitor become the industry standard for its products and services?	
How else could this competitor threaten your business?	
What are the implications of this information on your organization's strategy?	

Assess other parts of the environment. Most people stop at customers and competition when they develop a strategy. The remainder of this section asks you to consider other areas, such as technology, regulators, capital markets, and labor markets. Complete the worksheet that follows.

Worksheet: Assessing the Environment—Beyond Customers and Competitors

	Key Trends And Changes	Implications For Strategy
Emerging technologies		
Emerging information systems		
Capital markets		
Government		
Supplier power and dynamics		
The labor market		

Assess Strengths and Weaknesses

After looking outside the organization, take some time to look within. What are the organization's key strengths and weaknesses? What has been working and what has not? The following worksheet will help you with this assessment.

Worksheet: Assess the Organization's Key Strengths and Weaknesses

	Specific Strengths	Specific Weaknesses
Service		
Quality		
Cost/Productivity		
Speed		
Innovation		
Understanding of customer needs		
Customer loyalty		
Proprietary technology		
Alignment of executive team		
Information systems		
Strategic alliances		
Scale/Size		

	Specific Strengths	Specific Weaknesses
Sales and distribution channels		
Operational efficiency and excellence		
Financial situation		
Financial controls and systems		
Marketing strategy and execution		
Recruiting, retaining, and developing top people		
Human resources systems		
Products and services		
Other strengths and weaknesses		

Now answer the following questions:

Name up to three major achievements in the past year, and why they were successful.

Name up to three major failures in the past year, and lessons learned from them.

List key implications from this worksheet on the organization's strategy.

Choose What Your Organization Should Do Best

Great organizations do one thing—and only one thing—better than any other organization. They do everything else well enough to meet their customers' expectations. Meanwhile, mediocre organizations try to do it all. They stretch their attention and resources too thin, until more focused organizations beat them by offering better solutions to the same customers.

This section challenges you to pick one, and only one, strategic area in which to excel. It does this by listing eight common areas of strategic focus, and challenging you to pick one of them. The area you pick determines what your organization will do better than any other organization. It will also determine how your organization invests its time, attention, and resources. The key is to identify, and then focus on, one area above all others.

The eight areas include:

1. ***Product leadership.*** Companies who excel in product leadership become experts at developing and marketing a single type of product that leads in the marketplace. For instance, Nike® attempts to offer the best-quality athletic products available. Toyota® does this with cars, and Gallo® does this with wine. By choosing to be a product leader, an organization commits to innovative product development, strong sales and distribution, and outstanding service to customers.

2. ***Process and operational efficiency.*** Organizations in this category offer dependable products and/or services that customers can trust—all at a good value. Companies who focus on process and operational efficiency do three things well. First, they set standards that meet or exceed the expectations of their target customers. Second, they develop a highly focused and efficient manufacturing process or service delivery model to meet these standards. Third, they invest in systems and infrastructure to support their employees and continuously strengthen operations. Southwest Air®, McDonald's®, and Federal Express® top the list of companies in this category.

3. ***Ability to customize.*** Companies who excel at customization meet unique customer demands better than anybody else. These companies create flexible processes, hire employees who are innovative and can improvise on the spot, and celebrate people who go the extra mile to delight customers. Professional service firms known for developing leading-edge solutions, service organizations famous for meeting unique customer requests, and manufacturers who specialize in one-time orders excel at customization.

4. ***Proprietary knowledge and/or technology.*** Companies who succeed based on proprietary knowledge and/or technology develop processes, areas of expertise, or technologies that they offer to others. They sell their expertise through licensing, royalties, and consulting arrangements, or by embedding their technology in other company's products. Companies in this category recruit and reward experts in their field, invest heavily in research, find ways to adapt their discoveries to specific markets, and develop creative financial arrangements to offer their know-how to the market. RSA Security®, which developed a method for securing online transactions, and Velcro®, which developed a process for manufacturing a unique material, both fit into this category.

5 ***Excellence through sales, marketing, and/or distribution channels.*** Companies who excel in this area develop unique ways to market and distribute their products and services. Their sales, marketing, and/or distribution method builds powerful relationships with customers, and gives them a strong advantage in the market. For instance, E-bay® has become one of the most successful Internet commerce companies through its unique approach to matching buyers and sellers of merchandise. Bright Horizons®, a provider of childcare services, changed the dynamics of that industry by developing relationships with major employers rather than marketing directly to parents. Superstores like Home Depot® also use distribution as a way to gain a competitive edge.

6 ***Making deals.*** Companies that excel in making deals use their expertise in negotiating and creative financing to build unique capabilities. These companies typically include holding companies and venture capitalists. Companies that focus on making deals become experts at evaluating and structuring mergers, acquisitions, and alliances, and at maximizing the return on their investments.

7 ***Achieving scale.*** Companies that rely on developing scale find ways to get big to gain an advantage over the competition. A manufacturing firm might achieve scale by expanding capacity to drive down costs. A service firm might achieve scale by hiring a deep and broad pool of experts that nobody else can match. Scale might also mean huge visibility in the marketplace, or the ability to purchase large volumes at low cost from suppliers. Waste Management® is an example of a company built by buying numerous local garbage companies, and combining them into a colossal, powerful entity.

8 ***Sourcing.*** Companies in this category compete primarily on their ability to source supplies or products. Diamond companies, oil drillers, shipwreck hunters, and specialized importers often compete based on their ability to source supplies. They become better than anybody else at locating, and then acquiring, exclusive sources for their products and services.

This section continues on the next page. 

For many, the hardest part of developing an elegant strategy is choosing the one thing that their organization will do best. The following worksheet lists each of the eight areas of focus just discussed. Rank each area based on its importance to the organization today (1 = first priority; 8 = lowest priority). Then, rank each area again, this time based on how the organization should focus its strategy in the future.

This exercise might take a lot of time and discussion with others in your organization. The work you completed earlier in this chapter will also help you make your choices, as will your answers to the following questions:

1. Which area of focus matters most to your customers?
2. Which area of focus gives you a distinct advantage over the competition?
3. In which area of focus can you actually be the best?

Worksheet: Determining What You Should Do Best

Area Of Focus	Rank By Priority Of Organization Today (1 to 8)	Rank By Priority Of Organization Going Forward (1 to 8)
Product leadership		
Ability to customize		
Sales, marketing and/or distribution channels		
Achieving scale		

Finally, write what your organization should do best in your own words:

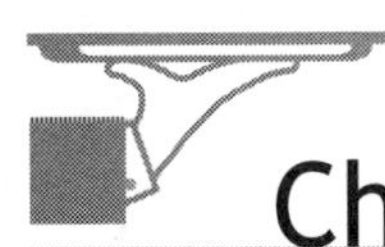

Choose Your Customers and How to Serve Them

Creating an elegant strategy forces you to make choices about which customers you will serve and with which products or services. For instance, Southwest Air® primarily serves customers who are price-conscious, make short flights, and do not expect frills. They do not serve international travelers, people who want reserved seats, or those who want to fly cross-country non-stop.

You already described your current and potential customers and services at the beginning of the chapter. However, now that you have chosen what your organization will do better than any other, think again about your target market and products. In this section, you will make clear choices about which customers you serve, and how you serve them.

Specifically, you will answer two questions:

- Who are your primary customers?
- What products and services will you offer them?

These questions are harder to answer than they may seem. That's because organizations must choose from among four possibilities.

Customer and Product Specialization Matrix

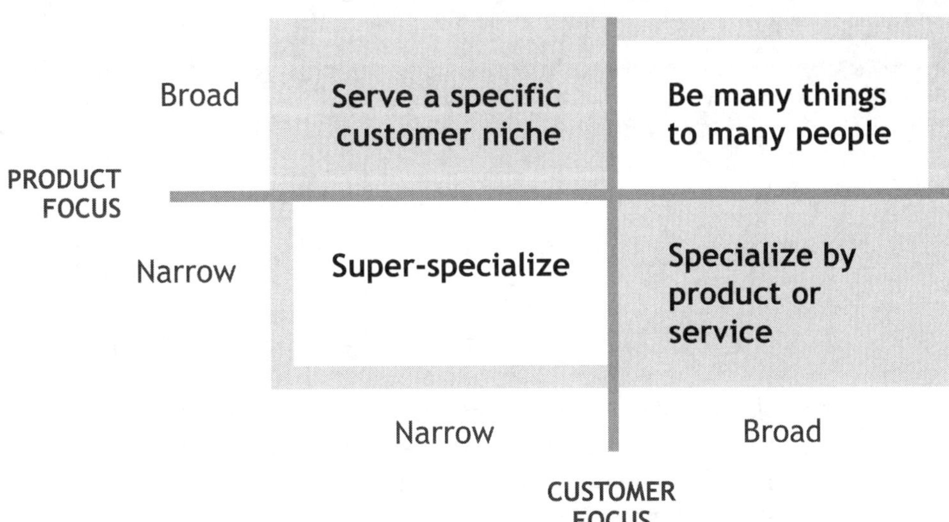

Super-specialize. Some organizations super-specialize, offering a specific product or service to a focused customer segment, such as a staffing firm that only provides software engineers to Fortune 500 financial institutions. Companies in this category might be perfectly happy with their niche. In fact, those that attempt to expand their products, or reach out to new markets, often pay a stiff price for their ambition.

Specialize by product and/or service. Organizations in this category offer a specific product or service, but market it to a fairly broad customer base. They adapt their products and/or services for each market they target. Nike® (athletic gear), Ford® (cars), and Dell® (computers) are examples.

Serve a specific customer niche. Some organizations offer a broad array of products and services, but focus on a specific customer segment. For instance, Eastern & Oriental® offers its luxury hotels, trains, restaurants, resorts, tours, souvenirs, and a magazine to high-end international travelers. Similarly, Home Depot® offers tens of thousands of products, installation services, and educational courses to the do-it-yourself home-repair market.

Offer many products and/or services to many types of customers. Some conglomerates, like General Electric®, have had success offering a wide range of products to a wide range of customers. However, most organizations that choose this approach wind up being mediocre, because they don't know how to focus on products and services specifically designed to meet their customers' needs.

It takes a lot of thought to determine which category your organization will choose. Would you prefer to be a big fish in a small pond, or be a small fish in an ocean? Complete the rest of this section to find out.

Who are your primary customers? In the worksheet below, define your primary customer, as well as the customer segments that you will either de-emphasize or no longer serve. Be disciplined about your choice—even if it means "firing" customers who are no longer profitable or who distract your organization from its main focus.

Worksheet: Choose Your Customers

Description Of Customer Segment(s) Your Organization Will Primarily Serve	Description Of Segment(s) That Will Receive Less Focus	Description Of Segment(s) That Your Organization Will Not Serve

What products and services will you offer? With these customers in mind, choose which products and services will best meet their needs, and which products and services your organization can phase out. These choices can be challenging, because your organization may have invested sizable sums in products that no longer fit your strategy or your customers' needs. By thinking about what you do best, and your primary customers, you can make the right choices.

Worksheet: Choose the Products and Services Your Organization Will Offer

Products And Services That Your Organization Will Develop	Products And Services That Your Organization Will Keep	Products And Services To Be Phased Out

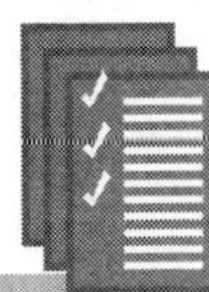

Choose Initiatives to Become the Best

You have chosen how your organization will excel, for which customers, and with which products. The next step is to identify initiatives to build your organization's internal capacity and, ultimately, to be the best in the industry. Identifying these key initiatives achieves three goals. First, it enables the organization to focus its resources on essential tactics and initiatives to lead the industry. Second, it shores up any weaknesses that must be corrected to meet customer requirements. Third, it points the entire organization in the same direction.

Based on your work so far, develop a set of initiatives that will help your organization become the best in its chosen area of focus. Use the following worksheet to develop this list.

Be sure that the initiatives you choose support what your organization will do best. For instance, if your organization will excel in product leadership, then most of your initiatives should lead to developing, marketing, and selling innovative products to your target industry. Similarly, if you chose to focus on process and operational efficiency, then initiatives should relate to setting standards for service, and putting systems and processes in place to meet those standards.

Worksheet: Strategic Initiatives

Department, Function, Or Business Unit	Key Initiative	How This Initiative Supports What The Organization Does Best
Marketing		
Sales		
Distribution		
Quality		
Human resources		
Finance and accounting		
Research and development		
Product development		
Manufacturing and operations		
Other:		
Other:		
Other:		

At the same time that your organization develops its ability to excel in a specific strategic area, it still has to meet basic market requirements across the board. It is no use being a leader in product development if your quality is unacceptable, or if costs are too high even for your most loyal customer.

The following worksheet provides a way to develop initiatives to address weaknesses in your organization. But be careful! The goal of this exercise is to meet minimum market requirements, not to distract your organization by having it do more than it reasonably can.

Worksheet: Addressing Key Weaknesses

Key Weaknesses The Organization Must Address To Be Competitive	Initiative(s) To Address Each Weakness

You have probably identified a large number of possible initiatives. At this point, prioritizing and focusing your organization's time and resources on a few critical initiatives makes sense. Of all of the initiatives that you have identified in this section, select up to five that your organization absolutely must complete to be successful. The rest can be completed as time and resources permit.

Worksheet: Top Five Initiatives

Outcome	By When	Person Responsible
1		
2		
3		
4		
5		

Choose Your Competitors and How to Beat Them

Now it is time to think about the competition. This section asks you to answer two questions:

- Who are your competitors?
- What tactics can you implement to beat your competitors?

Who are your competitors? In the space below, write down the organizations that you consider as competitors, given your new (or renewed) strategic focus.

Our key competitors will be:

1
2
3
4
5

What tactics can you implement to beat your competitors? Now that you have determined your competition, what tactics can you use to take market share from them? What can you do to fend off their attacks, and defend your turf? How can you attack their weaknesses and profit in the process? How can you anticipate their next move, and neutralize it? Use the following worksheet to answer these questions.

Worksheet: Competitive Tactics

Key Competitor(s)	Their Weaknesses And/Or Anticipated Moves	Tactics To Beat Them

Develop Messages for the Market

Part of strategy includes choosing messages to differentiate your organization in the market. Leading organizations communicate to their customers that they provide unique value compared to the competition. For instance, Oracle® frequently publicizes that it saved $1 billion using its own software, and that many of the largest companies in the world rely on their products. Six Flags® theme parks communicates that they have the scariest roller coasters, and that they are only a short drive away (compared to Disneyland®).

Choosing messages offers an opportunity to test your strategy. That's because a good message and a good strategy both meet three criteria:

1. A good message communicates the significant value that customers receive from your products and/or services.

2. A good message shows how your organization is unique compared to the competition, in a way that matters to customers.

3. Your organization can deliver what it promises in its message.

This section asks you to develop messages that meet these criteria. To do that, you will first come up with (or refine) key messages to the market. Second, you will identify tactics to reach your target market(s). Throughout this process, ask yourself whether your messages meet the above criteria. If they don't, either rethink your strategy, or rethink your messages.

Come up with key messages for customers. The worksheet below asks you to create a few key messages for your target market. Take some time to describe the value your organization creates, how it does it, and why you are unique.

Worksheet: Key Messages to Customers

The specific, measurable value your organization provides:	
How the organization does it:	
Why its solutions are unique compared to the competition:	

Develop tactics to reach the target market(s). Now that you have created your overall message, think about new ways to reach your target market. You can have the best message in the world, but without a way to reach out to your market, no one will hear you. In the space that follows, record ways in which you will continue to reach your target market(s), and brainstorm new ways to reach prospects. Ideas could include the entire gamut of marketing tactics, such as advertising, promotions and special offers, publicity, alliances with other companies, and face-to-face selling.

Worksheet: Tactics to Reach the Target Market(s)

Tactics The Organization Currently Uses And Will Continue To Use	New Tactics	Tactics The Organization Will Discontinue

Synthesize and Communicate the Strategy

By now, you have made all of the decisions you need to synthesize your strategy. This final section provides a simple, practical worksheet to summarize your strategy in a clear and powerful way. To complete this worksheet, you may have to have some final discussions with key people in your company.

Example: Elegant Strategy Worksheet

Our mission:	Develop the most ingenious and competitive racing bicycles on the planet.
Our vision:	In three years, we are renowned worldwide as the leading custom racing bicycle manufacturer. Every world-class bicyclist insists on using our brand. We are featured in every major bicycle enthusiast magazine.
Our values:	Be bold; do not compromise; have the heart of a champion.
What we do better than anybody else:	We customize the highest-performance racing bicycles in the industry for the world's most demanding racers.
We do this by:	We do this by working closely with the leading bicycle racers in the world, and by hiring the most talented engineers to customize bicycles to our customers' specifications.
Our customers:	Our customers are professional and amateur bicycle racers from around the world.
Our key products and services for these customers:	Our key products are customized and off-the-shelf racing bikes.
Our key competitors:	ABC Racing Company; Top Star Custom Bicycles; The Racer's Edge.
We will beat these competitors, and become the market leaders, by:	We will beat these competitors through endorsements and sponsorships from the top 20 bicyclists in the world, by sponsoring the world's most prestigious races, and by receiving awards for best bicycle designs from the leading industry publications.
Our top initiatives so we can continue to be the best and/or correct weaknesses:	Speed up our manufacturing cycle while maintaining quality; hire a fourth engineer; begin sponsoring up-and-coming racers; develop our fourth-generation racing bike.

Worksheet: Elegant Strategy

Our mission:	
Our vision:	
Our values:	
What we do better than anybody else:	
We do this by:	
Our customers:	
Our key products and services for these customers:	
Our key competitors:	
We will beat these competitors, and become the market leaders, by:	
Our top initiatives so we can continue to be the best and/or correct weaknesses:	

Communicate Simply & Powerfully

This entire book is about communication. From developing a strategy to strengthening relationships, from getting grounded to moving things forward, elegant leaders communicate simply and powerfully.

Furthermore, most of you already communicate effectively. You have probably received coaching in knowing your audience, setting goals, structuring logical arguments, and speaking in front of groups. When giving presentations, you tell your audience what you are going to tell them, then tell them, and finally tell them what you told them. You have learned that non-verbal communication accounts for as much as 93 percent of your message, and so you pay careful attention to your tone of voice and body language. You know about listening not just for the other person's words, but also for his or her emotions. Finally, you know firsthand that people interpret what they hear through many filters, so that communication requires extra clarity and precision.

Because most of this book is about communication, and because most readers of this book already know how to communicate effectively, this chapter focuses on five crucial themes that executives sometimes forget.

Be the message. Your actions communicate much more powerfully than your words. Under pressure, some executives send messages that hurt productivity and relationships. By being more conscientious of your communication during key times, you can be sure that your words and actions match up.

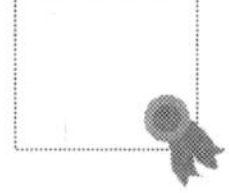

Be authentic. Rather than rely on "lovely lies," elegant leaders speak the truth, in a way that enables results and strengthens relationships. They also persuade colleagues to face the truth, even if it means giving tough feedback.

Listen with purpose. Most advice about listening focuses on listening actively and generously, while being emotionally intelligent. This section suggests an even more powerful way to listen. Specifically, elegant leaders listen with a purpose, and change how they listen based on the situation. That way, everybody gets heard and acknowledged, and results still happen.

Speak simply and powerfully. Elegant leaders synthesize information to come up with a few simple, powerful statements that enable people to remember and respond positively.

Treat employee communication as a critical process. At your organization, employee communication should be as important as marketing, cash collections, manufacturing, and research and development. Elegant leaders design both formal and informal communication mechanisms to make sure that everybody in the organization receives consistent, relevant information.

Be the Message

You communicate most powerfully in your organization through your daily actions. Words pale in comparison to how you make decisions, treat other people, react when the going gets tough, listen, give advice, deal with failure, support your people, keep your promises, and trust your people to do their job.

Few executives are conscientious of the messages they send through their daily routines and decisions, especially when under pressure. The worksheet that follows can make you more aware of the messages you may be communicating unintentionally. It does this by focusing on your behavior during challenging situations, and by asking you what messages these behaviors convey. Complete this worksheet (perhaps by asking some colleagues for feedback), and then answer the questions that follow.

Worksheet: Assessing Your Actual Messages

Question	Answer	Unintentional Message You Might Be Sending
How do you make tough decisions? How long do you take? How much information do you need?		
What is your tolerance for risk? How do you react to employees and colleagues who take risks?		
How do you react to failure and mistakes made by others?		
When do you give up and quit?		
How do you react to frequent and/or major change?		
How do you react to conflict, with or between, others?		
How willing are you to admit mistakes when you are wrong?		
How much do you trust others to get the job done?		
How much information are you willing to share with others about the organization?		

Question	Answer	Unintentional Message You Might Be Sending
How important is it for you to look good, be right, and have status?		
How well do your behaviors match up to the organization's stated values?		
What percentage of time do you keep your word (from being on time to keeping major promises)?		
When you don't get the results you had hoped for, do you blame others and hide from responsibility, complain, or use the situation as a learning experience?		
What percentage of your time do you spend talking about your customers?		
How do you behave with others when you are under pressure?		

Now, based on your completed worksheet, answer these questions:

What are some messages you may be communicating unintentionally in your organization? To whom specifically?

What is the cost of these messages to your organization and to you?

What, if any, behaviors will you change?

Be Authentic

In addition to communicating through your daily actions, you communicate most effectively by being authentic. Authenticity means speaking the truth, in a way that enables results and strengthens relationships.

First, to be authentic, you must be truthful. Many executives avoid facing harsh truths about their organization, and their performance, preferring instead to focus on "lovely lies." Common examples of lovely lies include:

- We are working together effectively. Why should we examine our teamwork?
- We will respond in time to any threats that the market sends our way.
- Our customers love us.
- We have a terrific relationship with the prospective client. This deal is ours to lose.
- We have a sustainable competitive advantage.
- The entire organization understands and supports our strategy.
- It's just a short-term market slump. We'll be out of it in no time.
- We'll succeed if we keep doing what we have been doing.
- My people know what I expect from them. I don't need to tell them.
- This will be the only round of layoffs.
- We treat our people as our most precious asset.

Speaking the truth means giving honest feedback about performance, disagreeing with ideas that seem ill conceived, identifying words and actions that don't match, and persuading colleagues to face potentially serious problems.

While being truthful is important, authenticity also means communicating in a way that gets results and strengthens relationships. Authentic leaders find the right time and place to speak the truth, and do it constructively. Authenticity does not mean being self-righteous, arrogant, or cynical. It means providing facts to support your point of view, and suggestions about how to move forward.

For instance:

- I want to examine our teamwork because I don't think we are working as effectively together as we could. We barely talk to each other, and when we do, it is curt and formal. I think we are uncomfortable working together.

- We can't keep doing what we have been doing. We need to test some new approaches quickly. We have to step out of our comfort zone if we want to succeed. Here's why...

- The prospective client has given us positive feedback. But I think he is saying the same things to our competitors, hoping to get some free consulting in the meantime. We need to do a better job differentiating ourselves from the competition if we want to win this deal.

Answer the following questions, and see how authentic you are at work:

What examples, if any, can you give of constructive feedback that you want to give to a colleague, but have not given? Why not?

What conflicts, if any, are you avoiding at work, even though you have something to contribute to the issue? How can you appropriately assert your point of view?

What examples, if any, can you give of a direction the organization is taking that you think might be wrong? How can you express your point of view?

Which of your professional relationships are weak because you have not been open and honest about the way the relationship is working? How can you strengthen the relationship by being more authentic?

What "lovely lies" does your organization pretend to believe? What is the cost of lying, rather than of telling the truth? How can you get the organization to tell the truth?

What other examples can you provide of inauthentic communication? What can you do to improve the situation?

Listen with Purpose

Elegant leaders don't merely listen; they listen with purpose. Depending on the situation, an elegant leader might listen with any of the following purposes:

Listen to listen, without fixing, judging, or interrupting. This type of listening can be effective at almost any time. It builds relationships, leads to deeper understanding, and lets people be heard.

Listen to understand the other person's interests, commitments, and aspirations. This type of listening helps a leader develop a mutually beneficial solution with another person. It also helps to understand somebody's reasons for resisting, complaining, or doubting an idea. For instance, "Joe, if I have heard you right, you're not complaining about this idea. You're just saying that you are committed to quality. Anything we do has to improve or maintain current levels of quality. Right?"

Listen for the other person's talents and interests. Listening for talents and interests allows a leader to point people in a direction that will engage and excite them. It also focuses on other people's unique gifts. For instance, "Mary, you're telling me that you enjoy meeting people, and are pretty good at convincing people to make an appointment with you. I agree. What would be a way for the organization to take advantage of these talents...?"

Listen for an opportunity to move things forward. Elegant leaders are brilliant at listening for ways to move things forward. When people keep talking about exciting visions and possibilities, elegant leaders ask them to commit to specific actions and accountability. When people seem stuck collecting and analyzing data, elegant leaders challenge them to make a recommendation. When people make commitments, but encounter hurdles and give up, elegant leaders encourage them to persist. When people identify problems, elegant leaders ask them to take responsibility for solving their problems. In this type of listening, leaders ask, "What can I ask or say to move people closer to results?" Chapter Twelve discusses this process in more detail.

Listen for opportunities to serve. This type of listening means keeping in mind the question, "How can I help?" It means encouraging and responding to requests for support, advice, and resources. It does not mean meddling, micro-managing, or offering unsolicited suggestions.

Listen for your impact. Often, we fail to have the impact on somebody that we had hoped. For instance, we want somebody to be inspired, and instead they are insulted or bored. Listening for your impact means asking questions and observing the other person to find out whether you achieved the result you wanted to achieve. For instance, you might ask, "I had wanted you to leave this meeting feeling acknowledged for how much you have contributed to our fourth quarter revenue. Was I successful?"

Now, answer the following questions:

Think of two challenging situations you face. What types of listening might help you improve the situation?

With which of the types of listening described in this section are you most comfortable? Least comfortable?

What other types of purposeful listening can you identify? How can those be useful to you?

Speak Simply and Powerfully

Leaders synthesize lots of information to come up with a few simple, powerful points. They remove data that is not needed, and rearrange relevant data in meaningful ways. While much of this book provides worksheets to help you think and then communicate simply and powerfully, this section serves as a refresher and reminder. It does that by introducing "The Rule of Up to Three."

The Rule of Up to Three provides a great test of your ability to speak and write elegantly. Since most people can absorb and retain about three points at a time, *The Rule of Up to Three* says that leaders should make no more than three points with each message. The rule encourages you to give no more than three reasons with every suggestion, have no more than three initiatives going at a time, and set no more than three goals for any one employee to achieve.

To test your ability to communicate simply and powerfully, complete the following exercises:

What are up to three things that your organization must do well to succeed in its market?

1

2

3

What are your organization's top three priorities during the next year?

1

2

3

What are up to three things you must do in order to succeed in your job?

1

2

3

What are up to three things that anybody who joins your organization must be, do, or have?

1

2

3

What are up to three characteristics of your target market?

1

2

3

What is the one thing that your organization does better than anybody else?

Treat Communication as a Critical Process

Great leaders over-communicate to employees. Communication becomes a critical process in their organization, much like recruiting, manufacturing, research and development, and marketing.

As the chart that follows shows, there are numerous ways to communicate to employees. Formats range from informally walking the halls to distributing company-wide memos. Purposes for communication range from celebrating results to solving complex problems. Some forms of communication start at the top of the organization and cascade down, once senior leadership is aligned. Other types flow from the front lines. Still other forms of communication rely on complex, informal networks.

Example: Communication Vehicles and Content

Communication Vehicle	Purpose Of Communication Is To:	What Gets Communicated
Walking the halls	Acknowledge	Results
Brown-bag lunches	Inform and update	Strategy
"Town hall" meetings	Communicate goals and strategy	Goals
Executive meetings	Share data	Initiatives
Management meetings	Celebrate	Budget
Staff meetings	Give feedback	Knowledge
All-hands meetings	Engage in a two-way dialogue	Values
Off-site retreats	Get advice	Vision
One-on-one meetings	Brainstorm	Mission
Broadcast e-mails	Collaborate	Roles and accountability
Internet site	Track progress	Standards and expectations
Newsletter	Solve problems and improve	Resources
Inserts in pay stubs	Learn and develop	Protocols
Information systems	Socialize	Norms and behaviors
Formal reports	Review performance	
Memos	Inspire and motivate	
	Apply pressure	
	State expectations	

Review the chart above, and answer the questions on the following page.

What additional formal communication mechanisms, if any, can your organization use to communicate more effectively with employees? Complete the chart below.

Vehicle	Purpose/Content	Target Audience	Frequency

What are key groups in your organization that should be communicating more effectively together? How can you improve communication among these groups? What issue or goal could drive the communication?

What are key messages and information that your organization communicates well? Poorly? How can you address the weak areas?

How can your organization's senior managers be more available and accessible to engage in dialogue with employees?

How can you facilitate improved informal communication in your organization? For instance, how can you help employees get to know one another better? How can you help employees make connections that will help the organization break down internal boundaries?

What else can you do to improve communication up, down, and across your organization?

Strengthen Your Power Base

Your network of professional relationships makes up your power base. You succeed or fail by the quality of these relationships. Some people make the mistake of assuming that professional relationships take care of themselves. As a result, they neglect to take conscious steps to rescue struggling relationships, strengthen neutral ones, and leverage strong ones. This chapter provides a way for you to be more aware of the professional relationships that matter most to you, and methods for improving them.

The chapter starts with the assumption that, in organizations, relationships are not based on unconditional love. Rather, they begin with an exchange of value, and thrive when two conditions are met:

1. Each person in the relationship offers value to the other.
2. Each person works effectively with the other.

Professional relationships won't last long if each party doesn't receive both business and personal value: business value enables each party to achieve their business goals and improve performance; personal value provides success, fun, challenge, personal growth, and/or increased status and power. In strong professional relationships, each person works hard to help the other person succeed.

People in strong relationships work effectively with one another, which is more an art than a science, and requires both parties to:

Build a bridge. We build a bridge when we care genuinely about the other person's concerns and goals; when we share values, experiences, and aspirations; when we acknowledge the other person's value and contributions; and when we admit mistakes and ask for support.

See the other person's potential. Instead of focusing on a person's mistakes or weaknesses, focus on their talents and ability to contribute in order to foster a positive and productive relationship.

Take responsibility for the quality of the relationship. When we take full responsibility for a professional relationship—instead of only our half—we can ensure that the relationship remains strong. Taking responsibility means owning the impact we have on the other person, regardless of our intent. It means creating an environment for open, honest, authentic, and respectful communication. It also means clearing up past mistakes, trusting the other person, and being worthy of the same in return.

Invest in and nurture the relationship. Like all relationships, professional relationships require time to develop and grow. By finding ways to stay in touch—in ways that add value—and by asking for advice about how to work together more effectively, leaders can continue to strengthen their professional relationships.

The above conditions rarely happen naturally. Building strong professional relationships requires a disciplined, proactive approach:

Identify your power base (the people who are key to your success).

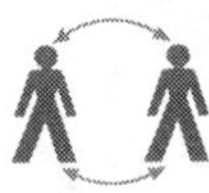

Assess your relationship with each of these people.

Understand each person.

Develop strategies and approaches to improve each relationship.

Create a specific action plan for each relationship.

Update each plan over time to continue to improve the relationship.

Identify Your Power Base

Your power base consists of the professional relationships that can help you succeed. This includes employees, colleagues, managers, suppliers, customers, advisors, mentors, and investors. It may also include friends, classmates, and acquaintances. It could also include people you don't know very well, or even at all, but should know better. In this section, you will identify the people you want as part of your power base. That way, you can focus on developing and improving your most important professional relationships.

Start with the list of key professional relationships that you created in the first chapter of this book. Review the list one more time, and compare it to your company's organizational chart. Think about outside consultants, advisors, suppliers, customers, and investors. Consider members of the press, leaders in the community, and various government officials. Add people who you don't yet know, but who could help you if you did—even if they seem "out of your league." If you want to, include the governor of your state, the president of the United States, the managing partner of the largest venture capital fund, the CEO of the largest company in the world, and anybody else that you think could help you. Finally, add to your list people who are important to your success, but that you don't like (or vice-versa).

When your list is complete, categorize each person into the following groups on the worksheet provided:

Strong supporters or mentors. These people are your biggest fans. They go out of their way to evangelize you, advise you, create opportunities for you, and support you during difficult times. They will even take personal risks to help you succeed.

Supporters and allies. These people think highly of you, trust your competence, and will give you positive references. They might not, however, take personal risks to help you succeed.

Neutral parties. These people are neither supporters nor antagonistic. You have a working relationship, and have not yet established the trust to take the relationship further.

Antagonists. These people don't particularly like you. They may feel threatened by your position, may not appreciate your style, or may have felt wronged by you in the past. You may work effectively with them from time to time, but overall, the relationship is not strong.

Nemeses. Nemeses go out of their way to speak poorly of you and impede your progress. They neither trust nor respect you.

Near strangers and new acquaintances. You have just begun to build a relationship and have had little contact with these people. They have only heard about you through the grapevine.

You are not on their radar screen. These people have never heard of you.

Write each person's name in one of the categories that follow.

Worksheet: Professional Relationships

Strong supporters and mentors:	
Supporters and allies:	
Neutral parties:	
Antagonists:	
Nemeses:	
Near strangers and new acquaintances:	
You are not on their radar screen:	

Assess Your Professional Relationships

Assessing your professional relationships provides you with important data for making improvements. Ideally, you should assess each and every professional relationship that matters, or could matter, to your success. For now, select the three to five relationships that you chose in the last section that either matter most, or that have the most opportunity for improvement. For each relationship, complete the assessment that follows. If you can, ask a colleague for his or her perceptions about the relationship. Even better—and, of course, this idea depends on the relationship—review the assessment with the actual person.

As you complete this assessment, think about the characteristics that you believe make a strong professional relationship. What insights do you have about how to improve your professional relationships in general? What can you do to focus more intentionally on strengthening your professional relationships?

For: ______________________________

Person's Name Here

Assessment: Key Professional Relationships

	Strongly Disagree	Disagree	Neutral	Agree	Strongly Agree
I am in contact with this person frequently enough to maintain and strengthen the relationship.	○	○	○	○	○
I involve this person in areas of mutual concern, and ask for advice about how to proceed.	○	○	○	○	○
I listen to, and acknowledge, the person's concerns and advice—even if I don't take the advice.	○	○	○	○	○
I understand the individual's personal and business commitments, aspirations, goals, and values.	○	○	○	○	○
When working with this person, I ask how I can help to achieve his or her commitments, aspirations, goals, and values—and try to do so.	○	○	○	○	○
The other person would tell me that he or she can count on me to keep my word and come through for them.	○	○	○	○	○
The other person would tell me that I have integrity and character.	○	○	○	○	○
I communicate effectively about how I have added value to him or her in the past.	○	○	○	○	○

	Strongly Disagree	Disagree	Neutral	Agree	Strongly Agree
I communicate effectively about how I can add value to him or her going forward.	○	○	○	○	○
I go out of my way to acknowledge the person for his or her contributions.	○	○	○	○	○
I ask for advice about how I can work and communicate more effectively with him or her.	○	○	○	○	○
I admit, and apologize for, mistakes that I have made while working with him or her.	○	○	○	○	○
I clearly state what I expect. This person knows whether he or she is meeting my expectations, and how to meet them going forward.	○	○	○	○	○
I have told the other person about my commitments, aspirations, and goals—and about how to add value to my work and career.	○	○	○	○	○
I harbor no resentment against this person. When an issue comes up, I either speak directly to him or her to resolve the issue, or I let it go.	○	○	○	○	○
I understand the other person's talents and gifts, and focus on those rather than on where he or she falls short.	○	○	○	○	○
The person trusts me enough to disclose sensitive information.	○	○	○	○	○
I believe that—when appropriate—this person speaks positively about my work and contributions.	○	○	○	○	○
The individual will go out of his or her way to support me, even if it means taking personal or political risk.	○	○	○	○	○
I would rate our business relationship as solid.	○	○	○	○	○
I would rate our personal relationship as solid.	○	○	○	○	○

Understand Each Person

The introduction to this chapter described two conditions of a great business relationship:

1. Each person in the relationship offers value to the other.
2. Each person works effectively with the other.

Building any relationship to have these conditions begins with a solid understanding of how the other person defines both personal and business value. It also helps to know more about the other person's style. That way, you can accept his or her style, and even adapt so that the other person feels more comfortable working with you. This section provides a tool to help you do that.

For the three to five relationships you chose in the previous section, take some time to understand more about how each person defines both personal and business value, and about his or her style. Answer the questions in the exercise that follows, using the example as a guide.

For: *George Smith*

Example: Understanding Each Person

Question	Illustrative Answer
What value does he or she bring to you? Why do you need the person on your side?	*George has significant contacts in the banking industry. He can provide introductions to some important prospects to help me build my business.*
What are his or her business goals? How does he or she define business value?	*George has an aggressive revenue target of $5 million in the next year. Business value to him is achieving that target while satisfying his customers and growing his division.*
What are his or her personal goals and aspirations?	*George wants to run the whole company one day. He also wants to be seen as an industry leader. He wants more time to be with his two sons while doing all of this.*
How would you describe his or her leadership and communication style?	*George gets right to the point. He doesn't like to make small talk, doesn't like to analyze much, and doesn't like emotions. He's a driver focused on the top and bottom line.*
How would you rate this person's tolerance for risk?	*George takes measured risks. He won't bet the company, but he is very willing to test and try new ideas.*

Question	Illustrative Answer
What criteria does he or she focus on when making decisions (e.g., technical, business, or political aspects, or process issues)?	*He looks at financial implications and return on investment first. Not technology, not politics.*
What are his or her talents and gifts?	*George is a natural leader, and very focused. He is brilliant when it comes to strategic thinking.*
What are guaranteed ways to anger and frustrate him or her?	*Ramble; have no point of view.*
Who influences this person? Who does he or she perceive to be mentors and trusted sources?	*Steve from the New York office has a great relationship with him.*
What past issues and resentments need to be resolved before the relationship can get stronger?	*George never forgave me for not including his division in the Chevron deal.*
What are his or her personal interests? How does he or she like to spend time outside of work?	*George loves adventure travel: skiing, scuba, sailing, kayaking. He also loves history books. He plays tennis.*

Now complete this worksheet on the following page about someone you know.

For: ______________________________
Person's Name Here

Worksheet: Understanding Each Person

Question	Answer
What value does he or she bring to you? Why do you need the person on your side?	
What are his or her business goals? How does he or she define business value?	
What are his or her personal goals and aspirations?	
How would you describe his or her leadership and communication style?	
How would you rate this person's tolerance for risk?	
What criteria does he or she focus on when making decisions (e.g., technical, business, or political aspects, or process issues)?	
What are his or her talents and gifts?	

Question	Answer
What are guaranteed ways to anger and frustrate him or her?	
Who influences this person? Who does he or she perceive to be mentors and trusted sources?	
What past issues and resentments need to be resolved before the relationship can get stronger?	
What are his or her personal interests? How does he or she like to spend time outside of work?	

Improve the Relationship

With a better understanding of the other person, it becomes much easier to develop a plan to strengthen the relationship. This section challenges you to think about strategies and approaches to improve the relationship, while the next section asks you to create a concrete action plan.

For the three to five people you have selected, complete the following worksheet, using the first example as a guide. If you are unsure of any answers, or find yourself making assumptions, speak with a trusted colleague who knows the other person well.

For: *George Smith*

Example: Strategies and Approaches to Improve the Relationship

Question	Illustrative Answer
What would you like the relationship to be like in ___ months?	*I would like the relationship to go from neutral/antagonistic to neutral/supportive, in the next three to six months. I would like us to refer business to one another.*
How can you adapt to his or her unique style of leadership, communication, and tolerance for risk?	*I need to more carefully consider what I want to say, and present it directly, with a specific point of view.*
What business value can you offer him or her? How?	*I can offer George referrals in my industry, as well as the time of some key experts in my business unit who can help him better serve his clients. Both will help him achieve his target.*
What personal value can you offer him or her? How?	*Helping George achieve his target will help him continue to be a good candidate to run the company. Giving him access to key experts will help him be perceived as the expert.*
How can you better acknowledge this person for the value he or she can offer, and has provided, to you?	*He's made some helpful comments before about how to run projects more smoothly. I never acknowledged him for that, and will.*
What are past issues that need to be repaired? How can you resolve them by taking responsibility, admitting mistakes, and/or asking for advice?	*I never took responsibility for excluding him from the Chevron deal. I will admit that, and ask his advice about how to inform him about deals that he might be interested in.*

Question	Illustrative Answer
What are some other things you can say or do to strengthen the relationship?	*Provide a two-page plan detailing what I can give him in terms of value through cross-referrals.*
What do you need to avoid saying or doing to keep the relationship solid?	*Not blame him for excluding me from key deals so far. Rather, show him the value to both of us of collaborating in the future.*
What are ways you can spend time with this person, whether at work or outside of work, to build the relationship?	*Initially, set up a meeting to discuss a more formal cross-referral program. George likes short e-mails over face-to-face meetings. That will be the most appropriate way to start.*
How much more, or less, time do you need to spend with this person to improve the relationship?	*We really haven't spoken much at all recently. I need an initial meeting, and then monthly follow-up meetings to measure the success of the cross-referral program.*
What are other ways you can build the relationship, without necessarily spending time face-to-face?	*Send him advance copies of our white papers; provide him with access to our in-house experts on oil and gas.*
How can you use your other contacts to build the relationship? Who does the person trust, whom you also know?	*I will ask Steve to give me advice about working with George, and to put in a good word.*
What other strategies or approaches can strengthen the relationship?	*N/A*

Now complete this worksheet on the following page. 

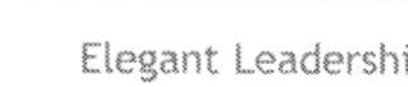

For: ______________________________

Person's Name Here

Worksheet: Strategies and Approaches to Improve the Relationship

Question	Answer
What would you like the relationship to be like in ___ months?	
How can you adapt to his or her unique style of leadership, communication, and tolerance for risk?	
What business value can you offer him or her? How?	
What personal value can you offer him or her? How?	
How can you better acknowledge this person for the value he or she can offer, and has provided, to you?	
What are past issues that need to be repaired? How can you resolve them by taking responsibility, admitting mistakes, and/or asking for advice?	
What are some other things you can say or do to strengthen the relationship?	
What do you need to avoid saying or doing to keep the relationship solid?	
What are ways you can spend time with this person, whether at work or outside of work, to build the relationship?	

Question	Answer
How much more, or less, time do you need to spend with this person to improve the relationship?	
What are other ways you can build the relationship, without necessarily spending time face-to-face?	
How can you use your other contacts to build the relationship? Who does the person trust, whom you also know?	
What other strategies or approaches can strengthen the relationship?	

Create a Plan to Strengthen the Relationship

At this point, for each person you chose, you should have a better understanding of the current relationship, how the other person defines business and personal value, his or her style, and some strategies and approaches for improving the relationship. Now you have the opportunity to create a thorough action plan. The template below will help you do that. Again, an example is provided.

As you make relationship planning a habit, you can jump straight to this plan, and save the other exercises for more complex or ambiguous relationships.

Example: Relationship Action Plan   For: *George Smith*

Question	Illustrative Answer
My six-month goal for the relationship:	*Develop a more positive relationship by agreeing to refer each other business in our respective industries.*
How I will measure whether I achieve the goal:	*I provide George with $500,000 in leads, and George provides me with same.*
Up to three things I will do to immediately strengthen the relationship:	*1. Apologize for excluding him from the Chevron deal, and ask for his advice about including him in the future. 2. Show the potential business we can gain by working more collaboratively and sharing leads. 3. Provide an overview of our internal experts, and offer to give him access to their expertise.*
Up to three things I will do to maintain and strengthen the relationship over time:	*1. Send advance copies of all white papers. 2. Send monthly update of all deals in the pipeline. 3. Create a report that tracks referrals.*
Ways that we will stay in touch:	*Monthly e-mails about the pipeline; bi-monthly meetings to review referrals; and monthly e-mails with advance copies of white papers.*
Ways that I will get advice about improving how we work together and bring mutual value to one another:	*1. Ask for his advice at our upcoming meeting. 2. Check in monthly by e-mail to ask for his advice—in the context of increasing referrals.*
Key messages I will use to communicate my value (or potential value):	*My unit does $3 million in business that overlaps with George's area of expertise. Of that, George could sell as much as an additional $1 million in services if we worked better together.*
Behaviors I will start using, change, or no longer use:	*I will get to the point with him, be more collaborative, and offer more information about our deal flow.*
Other ways I will strengthen the relationship:	*Like George, I also want to spend more time with family. As the relationship progresses, this might be a nice way to build common ground. I can also invite him (and his family) to my club for tennis.*

For: ______________________________
Person's Name Here

Worksheet: Relationship Action Plan

Question	Answer
My six-month goal for the relationship:	
How I will measure whether I achieve the goal:	
Up to three things I will do to immediately strengthen the relationship:	
Up to three things I will do to maintain and strengthen the relationship over time:	
Ways that we will stay in touch:	
Ways that I will get advice about improving how we work together and bring mutual value to one another:	
Key messages I will use to communicate my value (or potential value):	
Behaviors I will start using, change, or no longer use:	
Other ways I will strengthen the relationship:	

Develop an Ongoing Process

Relationship planning is an ongoing process. It is not enough to complete plans for a handful of people and stop there. Ideally, you should have a plan to strengthen the relationship for all of the people that are, or could be, keys to your success. At the same time, plans need updating every six months or year. And new plans need to be developed for new relationships.

This process does not need to consume much time—you don't need a formal plan for everybody with whom you work, or with whom you want to work. And once you have plans for key relationships, you don't need to completely revise all of them. Some relationships only need a tweak, or a little more face time. But by being more intentional about strengthening relationships, you have a greater chance of forging a strong, effective power base and of achieving your goals.

This final worksheet gives you a way to keep track of your relationships and your plans for strengthening them.

Worksheet: Ongoing Relationship Building Process

Name	Current State (e.g., Strong Supporter, Neutral, etc.)	Target State	Date Of First Formal Relationship Plan	How Often Plan Will Be Updated
Example: John Martin	*Not on his radar screen*	*Supporter*	*1/15*	*Quarterly*

Engage and Mobilize Employees

The last chapter discussed professional relationships in general. This chapter focuses on a specific and important relationship—your relationship with your direct reports. First, a personal story about the earliest days of my career:

For my first job after college, I joined an investment firm as an analyst. One day, three months after I started, the owner of the firm asked me, "Why is Ford's stock price down a point?"

I replied, "I don't know. My boss follows that stock, not me. He'll know."

The owner yelled, "What do you think this is, college? The next time I ask you about a stock, if you don't know the answer, I'll dangle you by your toes out the window...." He continued his tirade for 10 minutes, in front of most of the office staff, using more abusive language with every sentence.

Soon after, I took a job with a non-profit. During that year, my boss never gave me a performance review, never told me how I was doing, and never even gave me constructive criticism. When I asked for feedback, he said I was doing fine and changed the subject.

After business school, I returned to the for-profit sector, and went to work for an extremely profitable direct marketing firm. Four months into the job, I came up with an idea to improve the company. With excitement, I said to my boss, "I have an idea. I think we should—"

My boss cut me off. "You are paid to execute, not to think," he said.

Wondering if even one company existed with managers who knew how to motivate and mobilize people, I joined a management consulting firm. By working with many different companies, surely I would eventually find a company that employed managers who knew how to lead. While I found a few examples of outstanding leadership, I discovered that too many executives don't focus enough on how to engage and develop their employees.

This chapter describes a simple, elegant way to lead and mobilize employees using nine tactics:

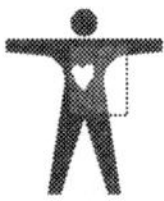

Know your employees.

Develop messages that engage and mobilize your employees.

Earn the right to lead.

Set clear expectations and tell employees how they are doing.

Tell stories that engage, inspire, and teach.

Customize your leadership to the individual.

Recognize and acknowledge each employee.

Develop employees for the future.

Get advice on how you can be better.

The sections that follow describe each tactic in more detail.

Know Your Employees

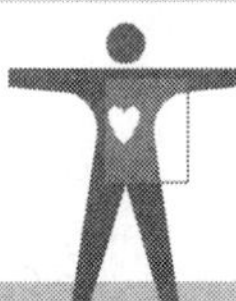

There are five crucial aspects you need to know about each of your direct reports:

Commitments. What are this person's aspirations? What are his or her personal and professional goals? What motivates him or her?

Values. What principles, norms, and behaviors are most important to the employee? How do those values fit your values and those of your organization?

Talents, gifts, and skills. What skills and talents does the employee possess? What aptitudes does he or she have? In what areas does he or she show potential? By knowing each person's talents, gifts, and skills, you can deploy your team successfully.

Style. There are many ways to assess an employee's style. How does he or she learn best—by doing, thinking, experimenting, or collaborating? How does he or she communicate—by asserting, convincing, involving, or inspiring? Does he or she get to the point, or tend to ramble? Is he or she driven by analysis, the bottom line, vision, and/or power? How well does he or she tolerate risk and change? How does he or she make decisions—by focusing on technical issues, business issues, or political issues? By knowing each person's style, you can better customize your approach, while helping your team learn how to work more effectively with your style.

Trajectory. Trajectory describes how far the employee can go in your organization. For instance, has the employee already reached a plateau? Is the employee in over his or her head? Is he or she a potential superstar? Does he or she have room to grow, but at a moderate rate? By knowing each person's trajectory, you can help your team members reach their optimal potential.

For each person you work with, elaborate on these areas. Use the template provided on the next page.

Employee Name: ______________________

Worksheet: Know Your Employees

Commitments	
Values	
Talents, gifts, and skills	
Style	
Trajectory	
Other insights	

Develop Messages that Engage and Mobilize

For people to respond to your leadership, they need to have pertinent reasons for doing what they do. They also need to have context—where the organization has been, where it is going, and how it will get there. With this context, they will understand how they fit into the larger picture, and how they can contribute to something bigger than themselves.

This section challenges you to come up with a simple set of messages to engage and mobilize your direct reports. There are nine core messages that, taken as a whole, provide the starting point for a two-way conversation with your team. Over time, they become the foundation of a shared mission, vision, and action plan that your people have helped to build.

1. ***History/Closure:*** "Here's where we've been and what we've achieved. This is our shared history together, and the history of the organization. What do we have to clear up before we move on? What do we need to acknowledge and celebrate?"
2. ***Vision:*** "Here's where we are going. How would you build on this vision?"
3. ***Mission:*** "Here's why we are doing it. Is this compelling enough to get you out of bed in the morning? What mission do you see us working toward?"
4. ***Values:*** "Here's how I would like us to 'be' as we get there. These are the principles about working together that we hold dear. How do they fit with your personal values?"
5. ***Strategies and initiatives:*** "Broadly speaking, here's how we will get there. I still need you to help me figure out the 'how' in your area of accountability."
6. ***Objectives:*** "Here are the specific metrics by which the organization defines performance. These are the results we will achieve, internally, for customers, for shareholders, and for other constituents."
7. ***Commitment:*** "What are your reasons for doing this? What are your aspirations? How do they fit with the above?"
8. ***Accountability and roles:*** "Given your talents and aspirations and what the organization needs, here is what I want you to achieve, and why it's important to all of the above."
9. ***Support:*** "What support do you need from me to succeed in your role? What resources do you need from the company? What else do you need?"

In my experience as an executive coach, I've found four types of executives.

The first type does an outstanding job of discussing mission, vision, and values. However, this executive fails to engage employees about specific goals and accountability. His or her employees feel inspired, but aren't sure what to do next.

The second type of executive has the opposite approach. His or her people know exactly what the goals are and what they need to do. However, this executive doesn't help people understand the big picture, how they fit into it, and why they should care. As a result, people who work for him or her feel like soldiers in an army, blindly carrying out orders.

The third type of executive lets people know the vision and mission, and also does a thorough job of letting them know what they need to do and how they fit into the big picture. However, he or she then abdicates responsibility, and offers little or no support to help people succeed.

Finally, the fourth type of executive uses all of the nine messages except history/closure. He or she keeps driving people toward the next milestone; however, this executive neglects to remind people where they have been, to acknowledge them for their tremendous contribution and achievements to date, and to clear up past issues that have created ill will. People who work for him or her eventually experience burn out, feel under-appreciated, or gradually build up so much resentment that they move on.

Given the above descriptions of each message and of the four types of executives, develop key messages that will help you engage and mobilize employees. Use the template provided in this section, including the example, as a guide. Messages can be statements, questions, or a combination of both.

As you complete the exercise, ask yourself these questions:

1. Which messages do I tend to ignore or avoid?
2. Which messages need to be clearer to have greater impact?
3. How often do I need to repeat each message to make my point?
4. How closely does each message connect to each of my direct reports?
5. What, if anything, will I do differently as a result of this exercise?

This section continues on the following page.

Example: Messages that Engage and Mobilize Others

General Message	Your Message
History/Closure	*It seems like only yesterday we were sitting around my living room table talking about starting this business. Now—in only three years—we have 50 employees and $50 million in capital. Before I tell you where we are going, I want to do two things. First, let's take some time to acknowledge our accomplishments. Second, last quarter was the first time we didn't meet our goals. Let's talk about it, learn from it, and put it behind us....*
Vision	*In three years, we will be famous for developing two new drugs to cure cancer. We will be known worldwide for our pioneering approach to drug development, and for transforming the way pharmaceuticals are developed. Drug companies will not only want our products, but also our process for developing effective drugs. How does this vision sound to you? How would you build on it? What would you change? What part is most exciting?*
Mission	*We are here to cure diseases that people once thought incurable. Is this a mission that works for you? Is it compelling enough?*
Values	*We are all about innovation, brilliance, and creativity. We will work around the clock to get results. How do your values fit with these?*
Strategies and initiatives	*Our strategy is to build on our unique technical expertise by hiring the smartest people and using our special process. Ongoing initiatives include drug development, recruiting great people, and forming partnerships with other companies to distribute our product and process.*
Objectives	*Our corporate goals are to: hire 20 leading researchers by June, move one drug through the next layer of the approval process by July, begin clinical trials with the other by November, and form a distribution partnership with Merck by December. We will also raise an additional $50 million in cash by the end of the year.*
Commitment	*Joe, tell me more about why you are here. What are your career goals? What do you hope to accomplish?*
Accountability and roles	*Given your interests—and skills—in strategic alliances and in making deals, you could play a key role in helping form the partnership with Merck, and in helping to raise more money.... Let's talk about specifics....*
Support	*What do you need from me and from the company to help you do this?*

Employee Name: ______________________

Worksheet: Messages that Engage and Mobilize Others

General Message	Your Message
History/Closure	
Vision	
Mission	
Values	
Strategies and initiatives	
Objectives	
Commitment	
Accountability and roles	
Support	

Earn the Right to Lead

Your position alone does not grant you the right to lead. You earn your leadership with every sentence you utter, every decision you make, and every action you take. Competence, credibility, commitment, character, resilience, and service are abilities that earn you the right to lead.

Rate yourself on the qualities that follow, which partly determine your right to lead. If you can, ask a few of your peers for their impression of how your direct reports perceive you. If you really have courage, have an objective outsider survey your direct reports.

Worksheet: Earning the Right to Lead

My direct reports would say:	Strongly Disagree	Disagree	Neutral	Agree	Strongly Agree
	○	○	○	○	○
I am credible. I have a track record that shows I can get results.	○	○	○	○	○
	○	○	○	○	○
I have character and integrity. The people who report to me trust me to do what is right, to keep my word, and to operate from a set of principles.	○	○	○	○	○
	○	○	○	○	○
I am resilient. Under extreme pressure, and in the face of considerable setbacks, I remain calm, am a source of strength and resolve, and find a way to bounce back.	○	○	○	○	○
	○	○	○	○	○

Based on your findings from the survey, what *one* area could use improvement? What actions can you take, what behaviors can you change, and what attitudes can you shift, in order to improve?

Fill in your answers below.

One area of improvement:

Specific people who report to me from whom I need to earn the right to lead:

One behavior I can change immediately:

One attitude I can change immediately:

Set Clear Expectations and Give Feedback

On a regular basis, elegant leaders find ways to communicate expectations and give feedback to their employees. One way you'll demoralize employees is by failing to tell them what they are accountable for, how they are meeting expectations, how they can improve, and the consequences if they do/don't. Some leaders meet weekly or bi-weekly to formally review progress. Others rely on teachable moments—live situations to model effective behavior, or to use as case studies. Whatever the format, and however frequently, employees should have a clear indication of what you expect, and how they are doing.

Following is a simple worksheet you can use to set expectations and give feedback. The elements of the worksheet include:

Expectations. Expectations should cover not just performance, but also how you want him or her to communicate with you (e.g., every other week in a meeting, as needed by walking into your office, by e-mail every day), and your expectations about attitude and professionalism (e.g., treat clerical staff with more civility and respect).

How the employee is meeting your expectations, citing specific, recent examples. Tell the person what he or she is doing well.

How the employee is* not *meeting your expectations, citing specific, recent examples (if appropriate). It is essential to focus on behaviors that can be measured, and that are specific. "You are sloppy," is not appropriate. "You failed to proofread this advertisement correctly; there are three spelling errors," is better.

What (if anything) you want the employee to do differently, and by when. If you don't tell an employee what you want him or her to do differently, you probably won't see much change. Therefore, it is important to provide specific advice about how you want the employee to change. For instance, the following statement provides specific advice: "Going forward, I want you to be 100 percent sure there are no errors in any advertisements you review—whatever it takes."

What happens if the employee does or doesn't improve—in terms that matter to the individual (if appropriate). Most employees change their behavior when they understand the manager's expectations. However, some employees need incentives to change. Incentives should be appropriate for the situation (i.e., it would be extreme to say, "If you are one minute late again, I will fire you."). You can offer positive incentives, such as spending time as a coach/mentor, providing tools to help the employee succeed, and offering more challenging assignments when performance improves; or negative incentives, such as not covering for the employee's mistakes, decreasing his or her responsibilities, and spending less time coaching him or her.

An offer of support. Most employees want to do well but often the lack tools or resources to get the job done. By asking how you can help the employee succeed, and listening, you can create an environment that breeds effective performance.

The following worksheet should be used only as a guideline. There are many ways to give feedback and you should do so in a way that is authentic and appropriate for the situation. For instance, sometimes you can start with an offer of support—especially when performance has just begun to slip: "I notice that the last three days you have been coming about ten minutes late to our team meetings. What can I do to help you get here on time?" Similarly, sometimes you don't need to offer incentives; you know that feedback alone will influence the employee to improve. And sometimes all you need to do is tell the employee to keep doing more of the same.

Choose a member of your team to whom you will give feedback—either about overall performance, or about a recent event or behavior. An example follows:

You've been helping the team enormously with your analysis, vision, and knowledge of the market. But I don't like that you've been coming 15 to 20 minutes late to our team meetings. Starting with the meeting tomorrow, I'd like you to be on time. If you start coming on time, I'll let you take a more active role in leading the team and running these meetings. If you continue to show up late, I'll stop covering for you in front of the team. Now, is there anything I can do to help you come on time?

Employee Name: ____________________________

Worksheet: Instant Feedback

What I expect: • Outcomes and performance. • How you communicate with me and keep me informed. • Your professionalism and attitude.	
How you are meeting my expectations, and specific, recent examples to prove it.	
How you are *not* meeting my expectations, with examples.*	
What I want you to do differently, and by when.*	
What happens if you do.*	
What happens if you don't.*	
How can I support you in making this change?*	

* As appropriate.

Now, for each person who reports to you, decide how often you will meet with him or her to provide explicit feedback. Fill in the worksheet below.

Worksheet: Planning to Give Feedback

To Whom?	How Often?	What Format?	Starting When?

Tell Stories that Engage, Inspire, and Teach

Stories represent one of the most powerful tools a leader can use to teach and train future leaders. Howard Gardner, Noel Tichy, and many other management scholars have studied the ways in which great CEOs and leaders use stories to teach. Stories contain drama, conflict, and tension. They touch not just our minds, but also our hearts and spirits. We remember great stories because they connect to us as humans, and offer a much more effective way to communicate than abstract concepts and directives. For instance, in the example given in the previous section, a personal story might have been a more appropriate way to give feedback to the tardy employee:

> *You know, you and I are a lot alike. I used to focus on the big stuff—strategy, analysis, driving to results. I didn't pay as much attention to the little things, like showing up on time. One day, out of the blue, my boss promoted my colleague to the director position instead of me. He was less talented than me, but my boss told me that she needed someone she could rely on for the little things. Something as small as tardiness set my career back at least a year! I bring this up because I see you as having enormous potential, and I don't want to see the same thing happen to you. How can I support you in coming on time to these meetings?*

The following exercise challenges you to develop stories that you can use to more effectively teach and train your employees. For each case, develop a story and share it with a direct report or colleague. Make storytelling a regular practice as you try to get your point across to others.

Exercise: Tell Stories that Engage, Inspire, and Teach

1. Tell a story about how you overcame a difficult challenge or adversity. Apply that story to a current situation.
2. Tell a story about your biggest failure, and what you learned. Apply the story to give advice and support to somebody who recently experienced a setback.
3. Tell a story about a key lesson you learned that helped you become a better leader.
4. Tell a story about a team that you worked on and how it came together and succeeded, despite difficult circumstances.
5. Tell a story about the best leader you ever worked with, and what you learned.
6. Tell a story about the worst leader you ever worked with, and what you learned.
7. Tell a story that provides insights about your own shortcomings, and how people can work better with you.
8. Tell a story that shows others how the organization has evolved, and where it is going.
9. Tell a story about how someone you know had to learn a key lesson—one that will influence one of your direct reports to change his or her behavior.

Customize Your Leadership to the Individual

Many of us rely on one style of leadership. But different people and different situations call for different strategies. The following table gives you a powerful tool for adapting your style to each individual employee's needs. But be careful: your style cannot remain static, even with the same person. As each individual's needs—and the situation—changes, so should your style. One week someone may need skills training and careful supervision, while the next week he or she may be ready to work with minimal oversight.

In the table below, write the name of your direct reports in the appropriate box.

Worksheet: Planning to Give Feedback

Approach	Description	This Approach Fits... (Name Person)
Remove	The employee is not getting results, and/or has a poor attitude. You believe that the investment in directing or training him or her is not worth the trouble. And, either the work is deferrable or you can find a replacement.	
Redeploy	The person lacks the talents and skills to do his or her present job. However, the employee has other talents and/or skills, and could be redeployed to a job that is a better match with his or her capabilities.	
Direct and inspect	You cannot trust that the person has the talent or skills to get the job done. Also, you are not sure whether he or she is motivated to do the job. However, you are unwilling or unable to remove the person at this time. Tell the person specifically what you expect him or her to do. Confirm that he or she understands, and review his or her work frequently.	
Manage their expectations/ Provide training	The employee wants to do more than he or she is ready to do. Before taking on new responsibilities, this person needs to develop additional skills. You are willing to provide training, while adjusting his or her expectations.	
Re-engage	The employee has the talent and skills to do a great job. However, he or she seems bored or otherwise unmotivated. You are willing to find out why, and address the employee's issues in a way that re-engages him or her.	

Approach	Description	This Approach Fits... (Name Person)
Mentor/Advise	The person has the talent to do much more, and shows great promise. The employee also has expressed interest in taking on more responsibilities and seems to have the talent and skills to do so. Provide mentoring and opportunities to grow. Give specific advice, based on your experience in similar situations.	
Monitor results and ask if they need help	The person is doing great work, and remains motivated. You feel comfortable delegating work to him or her while making sure he or she remains engaged. Monitor results and ask how you can help.	

How does the approach you chose compare to the approach you are using now? What, if any, adjustments will you make in your approach with specific employees?

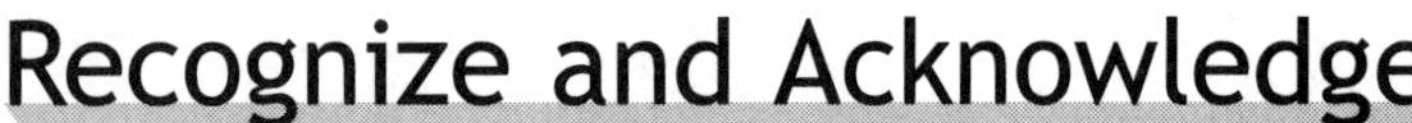

Recognize and Acknowledge

People thrive on acknowledgement and recognition. However, different people prefer to be recognized in different ways. Some prefer public displays, while others prefer private thanks. Some prefer monetary rewards, while others are perfectly satisfied with recognition that costs nothing.

The matrix below illustrates that there are four ways to recognize people:

1. Public acknowledgement that costs money.
2. Public acknowledgement that doesn't cost money.
3. Private acknowledgement that costs money.
4. Private acknowledgement that doesn't cost money.

Matrix: Recognition and Acknowledgement

	Public	Private
Costs Money	1 **Contests, Group Bonuses, Expensive Dinners**	3 **Give a Raise, Offer a Bonus, Buy a Personal Gift**
Costs Little Or No Money	2 **Pot-Luck Meals, Public Thanks, Silly Awards, Public Tracking of Progress**	4 **Private Thanks, Encouragement, Admitting Mistakes**

In the worksheet below, write the name of each of your direct reports in the box, or boxes, that corresponds with their preferred type of recognition. If you don't know, ask. You can write an employee's name up to four times, assuming that he or she is comfortable with all four approaches.

Worksheet: Assessing How Your Employees Like to Be Acknowledged

	Public Acknowledgement	Private Acknowledgement
Costs money		
Costs little or no money		

Based on this exercise, what do you learn about how best to recognize and reward each member of your team? What can you do differently? Many leaders may realize that they could spend a lot more time offering private acknowledgements to their employees. Others discover that they force their employees to tolerate annoying and tacky public awards ceremonies. Fill in your answers below.

Up to three ways I will change how I acknowledge employees:

1

2

3

Finally, using the worksheet below, identify those employees who have not been acknowledged recently and should be:

Worksheet: Employee Acknowledgement

Who	What I Want To Tell Him Or Her	How I Will Recognize Him Or Her	By When

Develop Employees for the Future

The more that you can connect your employees' work to their long-term goals and aspirations, the more likely you will be to engage them as members of your team. Moreover, the more you can help your employees grow and develop, the more you will be able to strengthen your team and move on to bigger challenges yourself.

Development planning offers a simple, powerful way to help both you and your employees think about the future. A development plan explains how an employee will grow professionally, and lays out a plan for him or her to follow.

A worksheet to create a development plan is provided in this section. It includes three parts: set long-term career goals, set interim goals, and plan to achieve goals. Let's explore each.

Set long-term career goals. These long-term goals represent the employee's overall career goals, even beyond their tenure at your organization. For instance, a long-term career goal for a manager in Silicon Valley might be, "To be a recognized expert in software company strategy and marketing."

Set interim goals. Interim goals (which typically have a six-month timeframe) help the employee achieve his or her long-term objectives, while helping the organization achieve its goals. You work together with the employee to arrive at goals that meet the needs of both.

Interim goals include:

- ***Performance.*** Specific results the employee will achieve.
- ***Initiatives.*** Specific projects the employee will complete.
- ***Attitudes/Behavior.*** Changes in behavior that the employee will make to be more effective and professional.
- ***Skills and Knowledge.*** New skills and knowledge that the employee will acquire.

Plan to achieve goals. The plan describes how the employee will achieve his or her interim goals. It includes some or all of the following:

- Assignments and challenges that will help the employee grow and get results.
- People, mentors, and new relationships that can help the employee succeed.
- Feedback and advice that will help the employee become more effective and learn how others perceive him or her.
- Formal training programs and conferences to make new contacts and learn.
- Affiliations and networks.
- Reading and self-study.
- Other resources that can help.

The process for completing development plans typically includes the following steps:

1. The employee develops a draft plan.
2. The two of you discuss the needs of the employee, the team, and the organization, as well as recent performance evaluations.
3. The employee revises the plan based on that discussion.
4. Each of you continues to discuss the plan and update it during monthly meetings.
5. During the next performance review cycle, the employee drafts a new plan.

If you don't already have a development planning process in your organization, create one today. Use the worksheet that follows to create an instant, elegant development plan for each of your direct reports.

Employee Name: ______________________________

Worksheet: Instant Development Plan

Long-term career goal:	
Interim Goals:	_____ months
Performance	
Initiatives	
Attitudes/Behavior	
Skills	
Knowledge	

Plan to Achieve Goals	Description	By When?
New assignments and challenges		
Meet key people, develop mentors, form new relationships		
Get feedback and advice		
Attend formal training programs/ conferences		
Join new organizations/networks		
Read and conduct self-study		
Other		

Get Advice On How You Can Be Better

Finally, elegant leaders constantly ask for advice—from direct reports as well as just about everyone else—about how they can be better.

Many leaders claim that they do this by asking for advice about how the organization can be better—better technology, processes, incentives, marketing. However, questions about the organization sidestep the question of whether you personally can improve.

Other leaders ask employees the right questions, but in ways that may never get an honest response. For instance, one executive announced at a staff meeting, "I'd really appreciate your feedback about how I can be better. My door is always open." How many employees showed up to give him feedback? None.

To get advice, ask specific questions like the ones that follow. Ask people in one-on-one meetings, not in large groups. Even better, have an objective outsider survey your direct reports for you. There are dozens of feedback tools you can use.

Key questions when asking for advice:

- What can I do to communicate more effectively with you?
- What can I do to more effectively clarify your role and set expectations?
- How can I give you more effective feedback?
- What aspects of my style do not work for you?
- What is one behavior you would like me to change?
- What am I doing that is working well?
- How can I listen better to your ideas and opinions?
- What can I do that I am not doing now to help you succeed?
- How can I do a better job supporting your long-term development and success?

When you get the feedback, ask for more details as you need them, and thank the person for the feedback. (Never get defensive or argue with someone who has gone out on a limb to give you advice.)

Then, after you reflect on the feedback, admit any mistakes, set goals to improve, and continue to follow up to make sure you have achieved your goals.

Complete the following exercise:

1 Ask each of your direct reports at least one of the above questions about how you can be more effective.

2 Based on their answers, what is one behavior you can change?

3 When will you follow up and repeat the process?

Elegant Leadership from Below

I learned the hard way about the need to have a strong relationship with one's manager. The lesson began when I was standing in a supermarket checkout line, reading an article in a popular magazine. The title, as best I recall, asked the question, "Are you at risk to lose your job?" The author argued that executives who had large salaries but only a mediocre relationship with their manager were at the biggest risk of being laid off.

I gulped. I met those criteria! At the time, I was making good money working for a consulting firm, but my manager and I had some serious issues. On a business level, he and I disagreed about realistic performance goals and strategy for my business unit. Also, he rarely gave me feedback about my performance. When he had advice, he usually passed it on through his executive coach, or through the chief operating officer of the company. Rather than confront him about this issue, I let it slide. As a result, I began to resent him for not giving me feedback directly. Over time, I began to resent him for other issues, too—from his lack of knowledge about my area of expertise to his management style. Again, I let these issues slide.

Meanwhile, on a personal level, we had little or no relationship. For instance, while he frequently spent social time with his chief operating officer and senior vice president of business development, he and I rarely met after work. He invited these executives to discuss his most pressing business issues and left me out of this inner circle, even though I was responsible for half the business of the company! Although I raised this issue with him and asked to be included in these discussions, he declined. I simply hadn't earned his trust and confidence.

Sure enough, within a month of reading that article the economy began to falter, and my manager eliminated my position.

I had broken one of the most important rules of elegant leadership. I had not developed a strong relationship with my manager.

While I'm not sure whether he and I ever would have worked together effectively, I learned a lot of lessons about developing a relationship with one's manager. As the previous two chapters suggested, these lessons apply equally well to almost all of our professional relationships:

1. Our relationship with our manager depends on both a strong business and personal foundation.

2. It is up to each one of us to take full responsibility for the quality of the relationship with our manager.

3. To strengthen the relationship with our manager, we need to fully understand what he or she values—both professionally and personally—and help him or her succeed.

Even if you are the CEO, you still have a boss! It could be your biggest customer(s), members of the board, or some key employees. Therefore, everyone can benefit from taking time to assess their relationship with their manager, and how to improve it.

This section applies the material in the previous two chapters to your relationship with your manager. It does this in four steps:

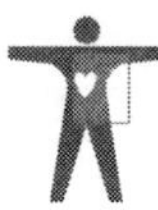

Understand your manager.

Assess your relationship with your manager.

Understand how you can strengthen the relationship.

Create an action plan.

Understand Your Manager

The following questions will help you better understand how your manager defines success, how he or she leads, and what motivates him or her. If you don't know the answer to any questions, either review them with a colleague, or plan a way to ask your manager directly. (If you feel uncomfortable having a conversation with your manager about how he or she defines success, then that says something about the quality of the relationship.)

Worksheet: Understand Your Manager

How does your manager define success in his or her role? What are his or her specific objectives and initiatives?	
How does your manager define success in his or her career? What are his or her professional aspirations and goals?	
How does your manager define personal success? What are his or her personal aspirations and goals?	
How would you describe your manager's communication and leadership style?	
How would you describe your manager's tolerance for risk and change?	
How does your manager make decisions—from a business, technical, political, aesthetic, or other perspective?	
What drives and motivates your manager to succeed?	
What are two or three behaviors or attitudes that are sure to frustrate and upset your manager?	

Assess Your Relationship with Your Manager

This section provides you with some key questions that will help you better understand and assess your relationship with your manager.

Worksheet: Assess Your Relationship with Your Manager

What does your manager expect you to achieve? What are five things you must do to meet his or her expectations? How well does your manager think you are doing?	
How does your manager expect you to communicate progress, results, and issues? How effectively does he or she think you are communicating?	
What does your manager expect in terms of your attitude, professionalism, and style? How well does he or she think you are meeting these expectations?	
How much trust and confidence does your manager have in you? How do you know?	
How well would your manager say you adapt to his or her style of communicating, working, and making decisions?	
How committed are you to helping your manager succeed—on both a professional and personal level? Would he or she agree?	
What, if any, past issues remain unresolved with your manager (e.g., failures, setbacks, conflicts, unspoken conversations, resentments, times when you let him or her down, or made him or her look bad)?	
Overall, how would you rate your relationship with your manager?	

Strengthen the Relationship

Now that you understand your manager and have assessed your relationship with him or her, identify actions you can take to strengthen the relationship and help your manager succeed.

Worksheet: Strengthen the Relationship

What do you need to ask your manager in order to find out more about how he or she views your performance and relationship?	
What can you do to help your manager look better in the organization?	
What can you do to prevent your manager from looking bad in the organization?	
What can you do to help your manager have more time to pursue his or her primary aspirations and interests?	
What can you do to communicate more effectively with your manager?	
How can you better adapt your style to work more effectively with your manager?	
How can you clear up any past mistakes or resentments that have been hurting the relationship?	
What judgments about your manager can you overcome to strengthen the relationship?	
What, if anything, can you do to improve the level of trust, respect, and confidence that your manager has in you?	
What, if anything, can you do to improve your personal relationship with your manager?	
What requests do you need to make of your manager to improve both your own performance, and help him or her succeed?	
How can you better communicate the value you bring to your manager and to the organization?	

Create an Action Plan

Based on your answers in each of the above sections, create a specific action plan to improve your relationship with your manager and to help him or her succeed.

Worksheet: Action Plan

Questions I Will Ask My Manager About My Performance	By When?

Areas Where I Will Take Responsibility And Clear Up Past Issues—Either By Letting The Past Go Or By Admitting Mistakes	By When?

What I Will Do Differently To Help My Manager Succeed Professionally And Personally	By When?

Other Action Steps I Will Take To Improve The Relationship	By When?

Think Comprehensively

While it is true that elegant leaders surround themselves with smart people, they still think comprehensively about issues and problems. When others see only part of an issue, come up with a narrow-minded solution, or take action without thinking at all, elegant leaders see the larger picture. They consider ways that different processes and people relate, and how one idea affects another. As a result, they find creative, thorough ways to solve problems.

This chapter provides a four-step process to help you think comprehensively:

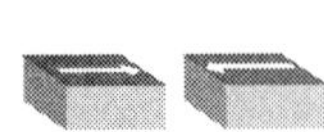

Define the problem. Some executives will jump right to collecting and analyzing data or, worse, come up with a solution before they have even identified the problem. Similarly, many organizations move in conflicting directions because leadership hasn't agreed which problems they want to solve. Defining a problem means clearly stating how things are, how things should be, and the gap between the two.

Create a framework for solving the problem. With the problem defined, the next step is to develop a comprehensive, logical framework that identifies potential causes and solutions. An elegant framework considers all relevant ideas, and structures them in a way that is simple and practical.

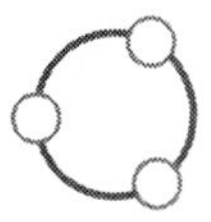

Consider the entire system. Most organizational problems are complex. Thinking comprehensively requires considering the whole system, and how the parts relate. To do this, leaders reflect carefully. They also involve experts and stakeholders in a dialogue about the issues, and revise their frameworks based on new perspectives.

Test ideas and decide. With a framework that considers the entire system in place, the final step is to test ideas and make a decision. This process is similar to the scientific method, and involves developing hypotheses, devising a test, and analyzing results. By following this method efficiently, leaders can quickly determine which ideas to keep, and which to discard. They can then decide what action to take to solve the problem.

While these four steps will help you think comprehensively, they cannot provide you with all of the information you need to make guaranteed-safe decisions. No process can do that. Eventually, you have to make difficult decisions, even if this feels uncomfortable. As a leader, you need to find the right balance between too much thinking and too little. As you read this chapter, ask yourself, "How much data do I really need to make a decision and take action?"

Define the Problem

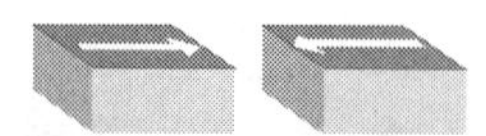

If you don't define your problem clearly, you can't solve it. As obvious as this sounds, many executives rush to provide an answer before understanding the question. This section provides a simple way to define any problem.

First, what is a problem? A problem is any situation in which things are not the way you would like them to be. In addition, a problem has a solution; the solution may not be clear, but there is a high probability that it exists.

A good problem definition meets three criteria:

1. It defines the way things are today, in specific and measurable terms.
2. It defines the way you want things to be in the future, in specific and measurable terms.
3. It sets a deadline.

These criteria are important. If you can define your current situation, and the way you want things to be, then you can define the gap between the two, fill the gap, and solve your problem.

Examples of good and bad problem definitions appear in the following chart:

Poor Problem Definition	What's Wrong With It	Better Problem Definition
We need to increase sales.	Too vague; no deadline; not measurable.	We need to increase sales from $1,000,000 last year to $1,500,000 by the end of this year.
John has a bad attitude.	Not specific and measurable; does not specify how things should be in the future.	I want John to go from making negative comments during our management meetings, to making only constructive suggestions. I want him to start immediately.
We need to decrease errors from 10 per 100,000 orders to five per 100,000.	Needs a deadline.	We need to decrease errors from 10 per 100,000 orders to five per 100,000 by June 30.

Think about some current issues you face. Construct clear problem statements that show how things are, how you want them to be, and the gap between the two. Use the worksheet below.

Worksheet: Defining Problems Clearly

How Things Are Today	How You Want Things To Be	By When

Create a Framework for Solving the Problem

With the problem clearly defined, you now have identified the gap between where you are and where you want to be. The next step is to determine how to fill this gap. An effective way to do this is to create a comprehensive framework of possible solutions. By creating a framework instead of rushing to a single answer or action plan, you can consider more carefully the cause of the problem and how to solve it.

The first step in creating a framework is to brainstorm potential causes of the problem. For instance, suppose that profit margins in your organization have fallen. You have defined your problem as: "We need to increase pre-tax profit margin from three to five percent of sales by the end of the third quarter." By brainstorming potential causes for the gap, you might arrive at any of the following ideas:

- Improve information systems to provide real-time data to employees about costs.
- Change sales force incentives to consider margin in all commissions.
- Decrease the cost per unit of products.
- Renegotiate supply contracts.
- Conduct a marketing campaign to increase sales.
- Increase prices to make more money per product sold.
- Decrease prices to attract more customers and sell more products.
- Change quality standards to attract more customers.
- Train sales staff on new products.
- Create a new product to fill a gap in the market.
- Increase the size of the market by conducting a campaign to promote the industry (e.g., "Got Milk?").

While the above ideas are all potentially valid, there is no way to know if your list is comprehensive. Therefore, the next step is to organize the ideas into a logical framework. A framework starts by defining high-level issues, then logically branching out into more and more specific issues. When done correctly, an elegant framework comprehensively addresses all the possible and important issues that could be causing a problem.

Using the above example, the ideas seem to fall into two categories: ideas that help to increase sales, and ideas that help to decrease costs. Therefore, as the diagram on the following page shows, these two categories make up the first two branches of a logic tree.

Illustrative Logic Tree

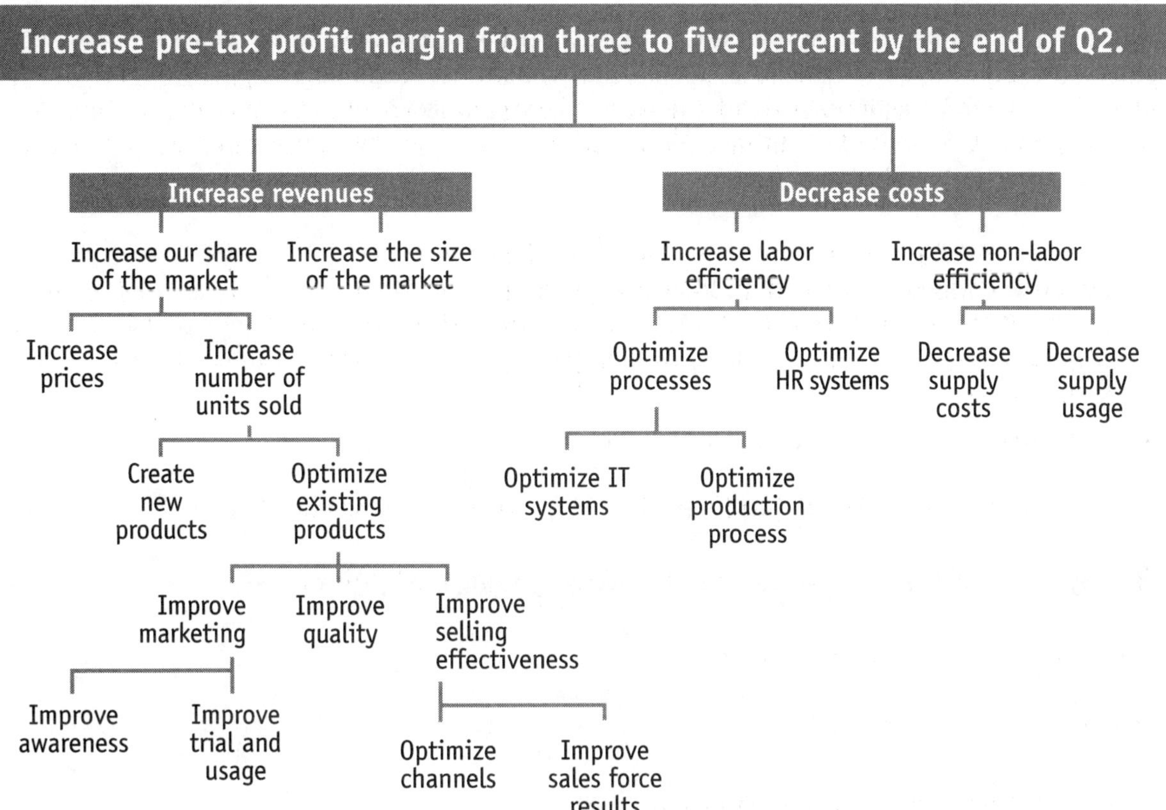

Additional branches in the diagram incorporate the other ideas in a structured, logical way. For instance, the way to increase revenue is by increasing the overall size of the market, and/or by increasing the organization's share of the market. The idea to promote the industry (the way that the milk industry's "Got Milk" campaign has done) falls under the category of increasing the overall size of the market. Meanwhile, the way to increase market share is by increasing the number of units sold, or by raising prices to capture a higher share of industry revenues. From there, ways to increase the number of units sold include optimizing revenue from existing products, and generating revenue from new products. The branches can extend as far as needed to reach the level of detail you want.

With this type of framework, leaders can much more easily consider different, more creative approaches for solving problems. They can ensure that they have thought of every viable idea, rather than rushing to the wrong conclusion.

The trick in developing a framework is to construct a logical structure that makes sense to you and your colleagues. Some executives do this instinctively, while others need help. Fortunately, thanks to a large supply of management books, executives can borrow all sorts of frameworks. Local bookstores and services that summarize management books provide most of the frameworks that you will ever need.

Remember—a framework only identifies potential issues and ideas in a more logical and useful way. In the sections that follow, you'll have the opportunity to flesh out ideas and determine which ones make the most sense.

Complete the following exercises to improve your ability to create frameworks:

1 For one of the problems you identified in the first section of this chapter, brainstorm a set of ideas, and then arrange them into a framework. What other ideas do you come up with as a result of creating a framework? Which ideas seem most viable?

2 Develop frameworks to address the following "generic" problems:

a Increase retention of top employees by 50 percent within two years.

b Improve customer loyalty by 50 percent within a year.

c Increase sales by 10 percent within a year.

d Decrease costs as a percentage of sales by 10 percent within a year.

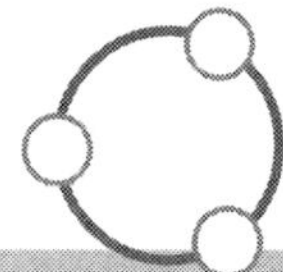

Consider the Entire System

Organizational problems are often so complex that leaders need to consider the entire system before reaching any conclusions. For instance, in the example from the previous section, any one idea might have a major impact on other parts of the organization: Introducing a new product or service might change the cost of manufacturing existing products; renegotiating supply contracts might reduce the quality of products, or the timeliness of shipments. These changes, in turn, might affect customer satisfaction and loyalty. Similarly, a marketing campaign to promote a specific product might change training and compensation requirements for the sales force. These consequences can ripple throughout an organization and cause serious problems if not anticipated.

Elegant leaders consider these potential consequences before making rash decisions. They do this by reflecting on their own, and by building models of the processes and structures that interact within (and often outside) their organizations. They also seek the advice of others for potential solutions to their problem. Involving others can be frustrating because they might have different agendas, incentives, and perspectives; however, by involving them early, you increase the chances of understanding how to work with them on this problem later, and of making large-scale change. You also increase the chances of discovering creative and potentially ground-breaking ideas.

Complete the following exercises. As you do, consider the problem you defined earlier in this chapter.

Exercise: Consider the Entire System

1 As you think about possible ways to solve your problem, what relationships among different parts of your organization should you consider? Which people, processes, and structures interact with others? How might these interactions create new issues when you try to solve your problem?

2 Draw a visual map of these relationships and interactions. What insights do you get once you have mapped out how different parts of the system interact? (See an example of a visual map on the following page.)

3 Who can bring different perspectives and new insights to your problem? What are their unique agendas and interests? How can you work with them to solve your problem, and help them succeed, too? What is the cost of not involving these people in the beginning?

4 When you have met with these people, adjust your framework to reflect any insights they provided.

This section continues with a simplified visual map example on the following page. 

Example: Visual Map

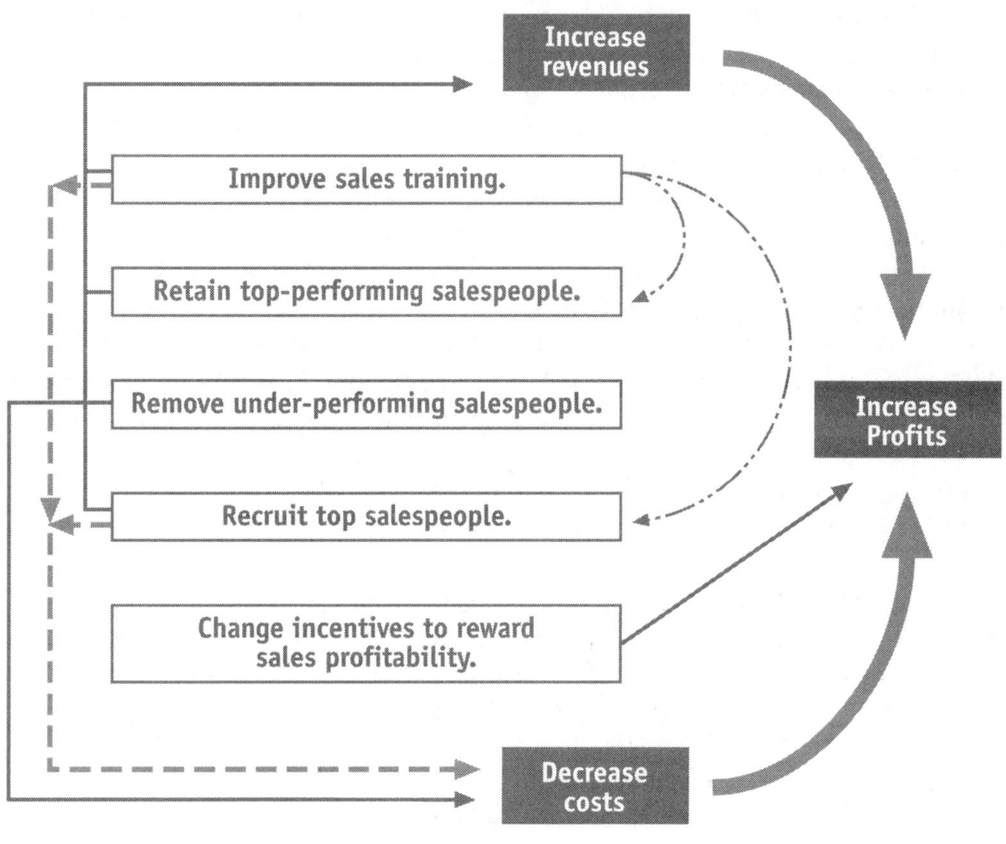

Key

Might temporarily increase costs.

Should decrease costs, increase revenues, or increase profits.

This idea also reinforces other ideas.

Test Your Ideas and Decide

Once you have thought about your problem and have involved others in the process, then you can test your ideas. By testing your ideas, you can get rid of the bad ones and build on the good ones. You can make a decision about how to solve your problem.

Testing business ideas takes four steps:

1. State your idea as a hypothesis.
2. Identify a way to test your hypothesis.
3. Collect and analyze data.
4. Determine whether the hypothesis is true or false.

First, a hypothesis is a statement that can be tested for truth. For instance, if you believe that raising prices will help increase your profit margin, your hypothesis might be, "A 10 percent increase in prices will lead to an additional $1,500,000 in pre-tax profits." This statement can be tested to determine whether increasing prices generates more pre-tax profits at all, and by how much.

Once you develop your hypothesis, there are many ways to test whether it is true or false: reviewing relevant past experience, conducting a pilot program, interviewing your target audience, asking experts, and/or creating models or spreadsheets. Tests don't have to take a long time, or be overly complicated, to get results. But by testing hypotheses in a reasonable way, you can be confident that your idea makes sense. Even the most creative, cutting-edge idea can be tested before the organization invests millions of dollars to roll it out.

Using your selected test, you can collect enough data to determine whether your hypothesis is true or not. If it is true, you can develop and roll out a solution. If it is false, you can test other viable ideas.

For any given problem, you can use the worksheet that follows to develop and test your hypotheses. Start by using the example on the next page as a guide. With the blank worksheet and the problem you defined at the start of this chapter, develop a set of hypotheses and a plan for testing them.

Example: Testing Ideas

Problem Statement: *Increase pre-tax profit margin from three to five percent within the year.*

Hypothesis To Test	How You Will Test The Hypothesis	Data Required To Test It	Source Of Data	By When The Test Will Be Complete
Raising prices 10 percent will increase sales by $1,500,000.	*Evaluate what happened to sales during the three previous price increases.*	*Volume and sales data, by product, during the three months preceding and following a price increase.*	*Marketing database.*	*June 30.*
Changing sales force compensation to focus on margin will contribute .5 percent to pre-tax margin.	*Explore three companies that partner with us, and who have shifted to a margin-based compensation system; pilot the system in our Northeast market for two months.*	*Sales and margin changes at our strategic partners; during the test, code sales booked by salesperson and analyze based on compensation scheme.*	*VP of sales at each of the companies; our Director of IT will create the data fields in our sales data-base during the test.*	*July 31.*
Our supplies are costing us too much. We can renegotiate our contracts and bring $500,000 in savings to our pre-tax profit line.	*Vendor by vendor analysis of price per unit, order volume, substitute and competitive products, and terms. Compare results to non-competing companies and industry database.*	*Line-by-line purchase order information, available from finance department. Industry data available from our industry association.*	*Finance department; our industry association.*	*July 31.*
A new product targeted to upscale consumers could generate $1,000,000 in pre-tax profit, and shift our margins up.	*Develop a mock-up of the product and conduct a focus group. If that works, roll out an early version of the product to three test stores.*	*Mock-up of the product; focus group data; if rolled out: sales volume of new product in test stores as well as data about any cannibalization of existing products.*	*To be collected during focus groups and limited tests.*	*November 30.*

Worksheet: Testing Ideas

Problem Statement:

Hypothesis To Test	How You Will Test The Hypothesis	Data Required To Test It	Source Of Data	By When The Test Will Be Complete

Now, with your hypotheses tested, what have you discovered about the cause of, and probable solutions for, your problem? What decisions can you make?

Successfully Influence Others

To lead, you must be able to influence others to think, speak, act, and feel differently. Without this skill, how can you get results or create positive change?

Influence is both science and art. It is science, because certain principles apply in almost any influence situation, certain strategies prove to be effective time and time again, and certain behaviors work better than others. Influence is also an art; for example, reading other people, thinking creatively, and responding spontaneously to others' concerns and issues.

This chapter provides a simple, powerful approach to help you hone the scientific side of influence. It offers an overview of the principles that drive successful influence, a process to follow when attempting to influence others, and a set of tools to choose effective goals and the right strategy.

The chapter covers:

Learn the principles of influence. This section introduces seven principles that enable influence.

Set goals. Without a goal, you don't know where you are going, how to get there, or if you have succeeded. This section provides examples of effective influence objectives.

Assess the situation. The more you know about the other person's motivations, as well as your own, the more likely you are to achieve your goal.

Find a hook. Once you understand the situation, there are four "hooks" that you can use to influence others. Some work better than others in different situations. This section provides an overview of each.

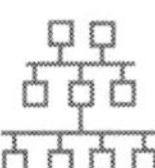

Structure the approach. Influencing others requires careful planning. This section provides a tool to help you effectively prepare to influence the other person.

Plan for the worst. Despite our best intentions, things sometimes go wrong. This section reminds you to plan for the worst, and be prepared to extricate yourself from difficult situations.

Rehearse. You have a much greater chance of uncovering flaws in your strategy, and avoiding ineffective comments, if you rehearse your approach before attempting it live.

Create an influence campaign. Most leaders must influence many people within an organization to accept new ideas and recommendations.

Principles of Influence

There are seven principles about influence:

1 ***People do things for their reasons, not your reasons.*** The key to influencing another person is to connect what you want with reasons, incentives, possibilities, interests, and commitments that matter to him or her. If you want your colleague to join you for Chinese food, you can talk about your craving for Chinese food. However, you have a much better chance of influencing her to join you if you talk about things that matter to her—her interest in trying new things, her love of spicy foods, or her desire to get away from the office.

2 ***Most leaders forget the first principle, and constantly need to be reminded of it.*** Time and again, executives forget that people do things for their reasons. As a result, other people perceive them to be poor listeners, overly aggressive, manipulative, and/or coercive. Keep reminding yourself of the first principle, until it becomes a habit.

3 ***If you don't explicitly ask for what you want, you probably won't get it.*** Influence happens through explicit conversations. No one can read your mind, and few people can "read between the lines."

4 ***Influence happens one person at a time.*** You can't influence Congress, the company, the board, or "them." However, you can influence Senator Joe Smith, the vice president of marketing, or the chairman of the finance committee. Influence happens person-by-person, conversation-by-conversation.

5 ***Take 100 percent responsibility for your impact on others.*** Just because you intended to get a point across doesn't mean you succeeded. Leaders take full responsibility for failing to have the impact that they intended to have. Rather than blame the other person for "not getting it," rather than becoming self-righteous, they adjust their approach and style.

6 ***Build relationships while getting results.*** Some people push so hard for results when influencing others that they come across as obnoxious, pushy, and dictatorial, damaging relationships with their forcefulness. Others tiptoe so softly when influencing others that they avoid productive conflict and tough issues—in their effort to preserve relationships, they sacrifice results. Effective influencers strengthen relationships at the same time that they get results.

7 ***In influence (as in life), there are no guarantees.*** When you attempt to influence another person, you might succeed or you might fail. If you fail, you might try again with a different approach, or you might decide to pick another battle. The most effective influencers do not take rejection personally. Rather, they realize that there are no guarantees, brush themselves off, learn how to do better next time, and move forward.

Set Goals

Influencing another person begins with a specific, measurable goal. Without a goal, you don't know where you are going, or whether you have succeeded or failed. Without a goal, you can't plan an approach to get the results you want to achieve.

Unfortunately, when influencing others, many people set no goals at all, or they set a vague goal. A good influence goal states clearly what the other person will do, say, think, or feel differently. It also can be measured, and has a deadline. Following are some examples of vague goals, and of specific and measurable goals.

Examples: Influence Goals

Vague Influence Goal	Effective Influence Goal
Joe will agree to be more involved in my project.	Joe will agree to spend two hours a week on my project, dedicate one full-time staff person, and attend the weekly update meeting. He will start next week.
Mary will be more supportive of my work.	Mary will agree to present an overview of my business unit's vision and mission to her staff at the next staff meeting. At that meeting, she will also publicly state her support for what we are doing to improve quality and service in the company.
Bob and I will work together to clarify decision-making protocols.	Bob will agree that I make all decisions about the creative aspects of production. He makes all decisions about finances. As long as I can show him that we are on time and within budget, he will release funds. He will agree to this when we meet on Monday.
Sue will donate money to our cause.	Sue will agree to donate $2,500 to our organization by the end of this month. The funds will be unrestricted.
Mark will stop being so annoying at the staff meeting.	Starting with the next staff meeting, Mark will come on time. He will also stop holding side conversations during those meetings, and he will stop making dismissive comments to people who offer a different point of view. Instead, he will listen to them, acknowledge their point, and engage in dialogue with them.

Think about a situation where you can use influence to achieve results. Who will you attempt to influence? What influence goal will tell you whether you succeeded? Use the following worksheet to set a specific, measurable, and time-bound goal.

Person to be influenced: ______________________

Worksheet: Setting Goals

What do you want this person to do differently?	
What do you want him or her to say?	
What would you like him or her to think?	
What would you like him or her to feel?	
By when?	

Assess the Situation

The first principle of influence is that people do things for their reasons, not for your reasons. By assessing a situation in advance, you increase your chances of identifying the other person's reasons. You can then prepare a strategy that helps the other person get what he or she wants, while you get what you want. You also become clearer about where you stand on some of the issues, and where you are willing to be flexible (or not).

The following worksheet provides a simple framework for assessing a situation. It starts by challenging you to understand the other person's motivations and interests, and then asks questions about your own positions and interests. By using this worksheet ahead of time, you can develop a stronger strategy and increase your chances of success during your actual attempt to influence the other person.

For the situation you chose in the previous section, answer the questions on the worksheet. As you complete the worksheet, consider these definitions:

- ***Motivations.*** People have different motivations in different situations. Motivations can include: status, prestige, credit, recognition, challenge, adventure, constant change, safety, security, popularity, looking good, not looking bad, money, time, freedom, self-expression, and autonomy.

- ***Reasons that matter to him or her.*** What reasons can you give to influence the other person to change? What benefits will the other person receive by doing what you want? What costs will they avoid?

- ***Incentives that you can provide.*** We control incentives that we can offer other people to influence them to change: money, time, public support, resources, advice, help, information, contacts, credit, friendship, and political cover.

- ***What you can take away, or use to apply pressure.*** We also control negative incentives that can influence people, such as refusing to cover for the other person, refusing to take blame, and escalating the situation.

Now complete the worksheet on the next page. What insights does it provide about how to successfully influence this person in this situation?

Worksheet: Assess the Situation

What will motivate him or her in this situation?	
What reasons might influence him or her? What benefits does the person receive by changing? What does he or she give up by not changing?	
What incentives can you provide, or offers can you make, that he or she would value?	
What can you take away, or use to apply pressure, that might influence him or her?	
What are his or her primary interests and concerns in this situation, and how can you acknowledge that you understand and respect them?	
How can you address his or her key interests, concerns, frustrations, and/or resentments before bringing up your own?	
On what points are you willing to be open to his or her ideas?	
On what points are you not willing to be flexible?	
What should you not say or do because it will escalate the situation or cause the other person to become unnecessarily upset and distracted?	

Find a Hook

If you assessed the situation accurately in the previous section, then you already have an excellent chance of influencing the other person successfully. The next step is to find a hook that will influence the other person to agree with your point of view.

There are four types of hooks, depending on the situation:

1. ***Logic.*** Logic includes facts, data, and reasons that matter to the other person, and that cause him or her to agree that, intellectually speaking, your suggestion makes sense. Logic works well when you are perceived as an expert, when the situation is open to rational debate, and when you are willing to be influenced by new information. Since reasons should matter to the person you are trying to influence, you will have the most impact by focusing on costs and benefits that directly relate to the other person. For instance, "Let's go out for Chinese food. You've shared that you want to get out of the office more for lunch, but only have 30 minutes. The Chinese restaurant next door offers a 15-minute guarantee, so time won't be a problem. Second, you said you were trying to eat light. This restaurant has a delicious light menu with 12 selections."

2. ***Incentives.*** Offering incentives works well when you are negotiating a mutually beneficial agreement, or when you want somebody to change their behavior to meet your expectations. Incentives are things that you control and that you can offer, or take away, from the other person.

   For example:

   Joe, my expectation is that board members contribute financially to the organization. While you've done a great job supporting the organization with your time, you haven't yet contributed any money, or raised funds from other people. I'd really appreciate it if you would either contribute $1,000 personally, or raise that amount from your contacts. If you agree to do that, I'll help you out with whatever support and advice you need to plan a fund raising event. I'll even put you in touch with our fundraising consultant. I'll also include your company's name in big letters on the sponsorship page of our annual report. If you don't agree, then I'll have to raise this issue with the board. It might mean that you become part of our advisory panel instead of being a full-fledged board member.

   In this example, no reasons are given. Rather, the speaker provides incentives that he controls, including support, advice, the offer to provide a consultant, and recognition. The influencer also offers a negative incentive by suggesting that the other person may not be able to remain on the board if he doesn't contribute financially.

3. ***A compelling vision of the future.*** At its best, a compelling vision results in inspiration, increased energy, and a shared sense of alignment and purpose. This hook works especially well when kicking off a new project, when re-engaging a tired colleague, and when encouraging a teammate to be resilient in the face of a setback. For instance, "Working together, we could transform the industry. We'll both be famous, sitting in our office on Park Avenue, our phones ringing 24 hours a day. What do you think is possible if we work together?" Notice that a compelling vision is shared; the other person can join in and build the vision with you.

Using a metaphor from history, sports, literature, or the movies—or telling a story about your personal experience—can achieve the same result. For instance, "We are like Sylvester Stallone in *Rocky*. We're bruised, it's late in the fight, but now we can show them what we are made of..."

It is important to use this hook only when there is a sense of common ground and relatedness. You and the other person should have shared aspirations, values, history, or at least complementary skills. If this piece is missing, your vision will seem glib.

4 ***Involvement.*** This powerful hook is essential when you need the other person's commitment to succeed. It means asking open-ended questions, listening, being completely authentic, and building a solution that engages the interests and aspirations of the other person. For instance, you might begin an approach by asking for help: "Joe, I'm really stuck. I thought I had let all of the board members know that one of their responsibilities is to contribute at least $1,000 per year. But, we have a week to go before this year is up, and I haven't received your check. Help me understand what's happening...."

Never involve the other person when you are not willing to be open and honest, or if you don't really want to hear their ideas. Otherwise, you will come across as manipulative and dishonest.

At the same time, when involving the other person, you don't need to be wishy-washy. You can shape and guide the conversation to introduce and test your own ideas—without manipulating. You can share concerns when you have legitimate issues about the other person's suggestions. You can focus on the other person's ideas that make the most sense to you. That way, the final outcome becomes a fusion of ideas and insights from both people, and both you and the other person leave committed to the same outcome and path.

For the influence situation you have chosen, which hook will resonate most strongly with the other person? Rank each type of hook in the worksheet that follows.

Worksheet: Prioritizing Potential Hooks

Possible Hooks	Ranking: Circle One (1 = weak; 5 = strong)				
Logic	1	2	3	4	5
Incentives	1	2	3	4	5
A compelling vision of the future	1	2	3	4	5
Involvement	1	2	3	4	5

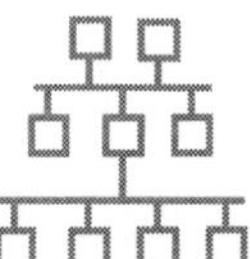

Structure the Approach

Now that you have chosen a hook to influence the other person, you can structure an optimal approach. The following worksheet helps you do that:

Worksheet: Structure Your Approach

State what you would like the other person to do, say, think, or feel.	
Depending on the hook you have chosen (pick one): • Provide up to three reasons that will convince the other person to agree with you. • Provide up to three incentives that you can offer the other person to comply with your request or expectations. • Share your vision of the future, tell a story, or use a metaphor that will generate enthusiasm and even inspire the other person. • Create some questions to involve the other person—for instance, by asking for help or advice.	
Anticipate how the other person might respond to your hook. What objections might they offer to your reasons or incentives? What concerns might they raise?	
What can you say or do to show the other person that you have heard and acknowledge his or her objections/concerns?	
What questions can you ask to more fully understand the other person's position and interests?	
Plan a response to the other person's comments. Depending on your hook (pick one): • Provide compelling reasons that address the other person's concerns/objections. • Offer incentives that solve the concerns that you think he or she will raise. • Adapt your vision so that it is more compelling to that person, and incorporates his or her aspirations. • Ask questions to involve the other person.	

What other concerns or objections might the other person raise?	
What other hooks can you offer in case the other person does not react favorably to your approach?	
What can you do during the meeting to make sure the other person is comfortable and that the professional relationship remains strong?	

Prepare for the Worst

Sometimes, things go wrong. The other person gets upset or angry. They present new information that changes the situation, bring in an "objective" observer or a supporter, or refuse to listen to you. You find yourself getting upset, or angry.

When things go wrong, the last thing you should do is remain in the situation. If you do, odds are excellent that things will spiral downward until both of you resent each other. If the other person gets visibly upset, stop pushing so hard and take a break. If the other person presents information that changes the situation, ask for some time to review it before the meeting continues. If you get upset, ask to take a break before saying something you will regret. If the other person seems completely inflexible, change your approach or excuse yourself to come up with a new approach for another time.

The best way to get out of a bad situation is by being honest:

- "It seems like we're not getting anywhere. How about if we take some time to cool down, and meet again tomorrow?"
- "You seem upset. Did I say something to upset you?...I'm sorry you feel this way. Should I come back tomorrow?"
- "I need to absorb this new information you've presented. Can you give me a couple of hours?"
- "I thought that only you and I were going to be meeting. I'd rather not have Joe here. If you insist that he be here, I'd rather reschedule for a time when you and I can meet first."

Take some time to anticipate what could go wrong in your upcoming influence situation. Answer the following questions:

1 What could go wrong?

2 What will you do if things go from bad to worse?

3 How will you excuse yourself and reschedule for another time?

Rehearse

When stakes are high, it makes sense to rehearse your approach rather than go in cold. Every time that I have worked with an executive to rehearse for an upcoming meeting, he or she had one or more insights about how to be more effective. In one case, an executive was prepared to go into the meeting blaming his colleague for poor financial results. When we rehearsed, he quickly saw that his approach would be disastrous and lead to a shouting match. By admitting his own mistakes up front, and then involving his colleague, he achieved his goals while strengthening the relationship.

Here's how you rehearse:

1. ***Find a partner.*** Choose somebody who can act like the person you want to influence.

2. ***Brief your partner about the situation, your goals, and how he or she should behave.***

3. ***Take a moment and blurt out everything you really want to say—the insults, curses, threats, and accusations.*** Yell, swear, and stomp your feet. Do whatever you need to do to get out all the inappropriate behaviors now.

4. ***Spend two minutes trying to influence the other person.*** Then stop, and get feedback about whether what you were doing was working. Give advice to the other person about how he or she can more effectively act the part. By stopping after only two minutes, you can get rapid feedback.

5. ***Start again from the beginning.*** Stop after three minutes. Get, and give, feedback.

6. ***Keep rehearsing, for at least 30 minutes.*** Stop every few minutes to review. From time to time, ask your partner to get tougher, or easier, so you can experiment. Change your own approach, to learn what works and what doesn't. Try an approach that you are absolutely sure will fail, and see what happens. Have your partner get upset, and implement the plan you prepared in the last section.

7. ***When you feel like you've covered every single possibility, take some time to recap what you learned.***

Whether you rehearse or not, you may not achieve your goal. However, if you rehearse and don't achieve your goal, at least you know that you did everything possible to succeed.

Exercise:
For the influence situation you have chosen, with whom will you rehearse? By when?

Create an Influence Campaign

Much of the time, leaders need to influence many people in order to make large-scale change. In this type of influence campaign, success depends on identifying the key people who have a say in your idea, and influencing enough people to make your idea happen.

When planning an influence campaign, you should be prepared to answer five questions:

1. ***Who are the key people that will be involved in this decision?***
2. ***What is each person's decision-making role?*** Roles could include: making the final decision, providing a recommendation, and providing input.
3. ***How much power does each person wield?*** In an influence campaign, different people wield different amounts of power. Often a person's formal title has little bearing on their actual power to make a decision about your issue. An executive might have no power, while a few front-line staff members might have all the say. By determining who has the power to make your idea succeed or fail, you will have a better idea about whom you need on your side.
4. ***For each person, how much does he or she support the idea?*** By knowing how much each person supports your idea (along with how much power they have), you can determine the overall likelihood of success.
5. ***Do enough people with enough power support the idea?*** If so, you can make your idea or initiative happen. If not, then you need to develop a strategy to build support.

Think about an idea or initiative you want to promote, or are promoting, in your organization. With that idea in mind, use the three worksheets in this section to help you develop an influence campaign. The first worksheet helps you assess whether you have enough support for your idea or initiative. It does that by asking you to list all of the people involved in the decision to move forward, along with a rating of how much power they wield, and how much they support your idea. The other two worksheets help you develop an action plan to get any additional support you might need, and to create an action plan.

Complete the first worksheet on the opposite page by filling in the information requested.

Worksheet: Assessing the Likelihood of Success

Names Of Key People Involved In The Decision	Each Person's Decision-Making Role In This Situation	How Much Power Does The Person Wield In This Situation?				How Much Does The Person Support The Idea?		
		None	Low	Medium	High	Resists	Neutral	Supports
		○	○	○	○	○	○	○
		○	○	○	○	○	○	○
		○	○	○	○	○	○	○
		○	○	○	○	○	○	○
		○	○	○	○	○	○	○
		○	○	○	○	○	○	○
		○	○	○	○	○	○	○
		○	○	○	○	○	○	○
		○	○	○	○	○	○	○
		○	○	○	○	○	○	○

Review the worksheet you just completed. Do you have enough support to make the idea succeed? If not, complete the next worksheet. It asks you to think about who else you need on your side for your idea to succeed, and how you will get them on your side. After you are done, complete the third worksheet, which provides a template for an action plan.

Worksheet: Strategy to Build Additional Support

Who Else You Need On Your Side	Who Is Best Suited To Influence This Person To Support Your Idea?	What Approach Will Influence This Person? *List Specific Hooks*	If The Person Can't Be Influenced To Support Your Idea, How Can You At Least Neutralize Or Isolate Him/Her?

Given your answers so far, create an action plan to complete a successful influence campaign. Use the worksheet provided. With this action plan completed, you now have an organized strategy to conduct your influence campaign.

Worksheet: Action Plan to Complete Influence Campaign

Key Person You Need To Influence	Who Will Influence Him Or Her?	By When?	With What Hook/Approach?

Move Things Forward

To get results, leaders move things forward. While less seasoned managers and executives move things forward through force of will, the most elegant leaders move things forward in such a way that others barely notice. They do this by building a foundation, based on much of the advice in this book. For instance, they remain grounded in their vision, and in their commitment to get results. Likewise, they create a clear strategy to achieve results. They also develop strong professional relationships that create a base of trust, credibility, and political capital from which to draw.

With this foundation in place, elegant leaders do four things to move things forward:

Surrender (more and more) to the process. Effective leaders understand that they control much less in their organizations than they would like. Rather than pretending to have complete control, they trust that employees and colleagues have the knowledge, expertise, and commitment to do what needs to be done. They also trust that people will organize themselves naturally in efficient and effective ways. These leaders don't abdicate responsibility; they still remain engaged, active, and accessible, striking the optimal balance between flexibility and rigidity in their organization.

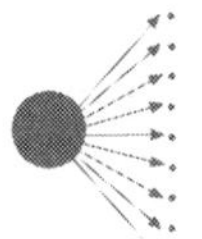

Shift the organization's focus. When the time is right, elegant leaders help employees, colleagues, and managers shift their focus to continue to move things forward. For instance, if employees are overly focused on collecting and analyzing data, the leader might encourage them to make a recommendation based on their analysis to date. In this sense, leaders observe and monitor, and serve as a catalyst when people are stuck.

Do not give up. When everyone else seems ready to quit, elegant leaders find ways to keep things going. They have tremendous staying power, partly because they understand that different people tend to give up at different times, in different ways. Some quit early in a project, perhaps after encountering initial resistance. Others give up in the middle, when it seems like the end will never arrive. Still others quit just before finishing, when a final push will achieve success. At the same time, some people keep moving forward, but make serious sacrifices—for instance, in relationships or integrity—in order to succeed. The elegant leader keeps persevering, in a way that is graceful and professional.

Overcome setbacks. Elegant leaders find creative ways to overcome serious setbacks. First, they anticipate and remove obstacles, often before they even arise. Second, they are extremely resourceful; when things go poorly, they find effective and unique ways to get back on track. Third, they overcome setbacks by remaining resilient, and by coping with continuous challenges and crises.

The remainder of this chapter considers each of these four capabilities in depth.

Surrender (More and More) to the Process

It may seem strange in a chapter about moving things forward to suggest that leaders should surrender. However, the fact is that much of what happens in our organizations remains out of our control. Employees and colleagues possess knowledge and expertise that we don't. Many processes are so complex, and interact with so many other processes, that any individual controls only a small piece. Similarly, projects can become so intricate and detailed, with so many dependencies, that no single person can control the outcome. We depend on formal and informal networks of individuals, each with their own interests and goals—each with their own authority—in order to succeed. Total control is an illusion.

Executives who believe that they control every task and outcome in the organization micro-manage and meddle, rather than trusting their employees to get the job done. They invalidate the knowledge and expertise of their colleagues, and refuse to collaborate or let others present valid ideas. When things get off track, they can create unnecessary stress and conflict, or blame others for issues. Worst of all, the illusion of control can cause executives to become fatigued, rushing around to dictate tasks and methods that others could figure out on their own. Eventually, this illusion can lead to lack of fulfillment and burn out—for the executive and his or her colleagues and employees.

The work of Margaret Wheatley, author of *Leadership and the New Science: Discovering Order in a Chaotic World*, suggests that people naturally organize themselves effectively. By facilitating this process, rather than interfering in it, leaders can free up their teams to achieve creative and powerful results. In this model, leaders guide, facilitate, and support. They also build strong professional relationships. They do not abdicate or shift responsibility, and still remain extremely active and engaged in the process. If things go significantly off track, they reinforce discipline and accountability. Finally, they make sure that the organization maintains a balance between being too rigid and bureaucratic, and being too chaotic. As one CEO said, "Over the years, I've learned that I can step back and let others take over. I don't need to control everything. In fact, when I've tried to control things I've made my biggest mistakes."

Leaders find the right balance between freedom and rigidity.

How willing are you to surrender to the process? How much do you trust your employees to get the job done? When should you step in and assert your control? How much control is too much?

Complete the following assessment to get a better understanding of your comfort with surrendering. Ask some colleagues and employees to validate your answers.

Self-Assessment: Willingness to Surrender to the Process

	No	Yes
I trust my employees and colleagues to do their piece and get the job done.	○	○
I respect and appreciate the talents and gifts of my employees and colleagues.	○	○
I understand that many things that take place in the organization are out of my direct control. I try to influence some things, and trust that other situations will work themselves out on their own.	○	○
I am open to being influenced when colleagues and employees have different ideas than I do about how things should get done. I don't need to dictate everything about completing a project or reaching a goal.	○	○
As long as employees and colleagues are on track, I don't offer unsolicited advice about how to do things.	○	○
My employees would not say that I meddle or micro-manage.	○	○
When I don't know something, or when I am stuck, I ask for help from others.	○	○
I realize that complete information rarely exists. I make decisions without complete information, in a timely way.	○	○

What insights did you have about your willingness to surrender (more and more) to the process? What changes can you make in your behavior?

Shift the Organization's Focus

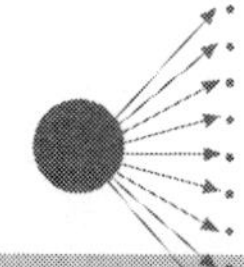

Elegant leaders move things forward by shifting the focus of their peers and employees. They recognize that organizations, teams, and projects progress through different stages. When the time is right, they shift how employees and colleagues focus their attention. In this sense, leaders observe and monitor, and serve as a catalyst when people are stuck.

The following chart shows different ways that individuals and teams focus their attention. Leaders provide support and guidance as needed while employees and colleagues focus on the specific areas shown below:

Leaders shift their organization's focus.

Leaders watch for the right time to shift focus from one area to another; for example, they help their teams, units, and organizations make the following shifts:

From negativity to developing vision and identifying opportunities. When employees and colleagues see no hope, complain about issues, or want to maintain the status quo, leaders shift them into more productive areas of focus. For instance, they might help employees develop a shared vision of the future—one that offers more exciting possibilities. Or they might start a dialogue to identify new opportunities and ideas to solve current problems.

From negativity to setting goals and assigning accountability. Another way for leaders to shift employees and colleagues out of negativity might be to have them take responsibility for fixing the problem they keep complaining about. For instance, the leader might say, "Thanks for bringing the problem to my attention. I'm happy to help you solve it, as soon as you come back to me with some reasonable recommendations about how to make it go away."

From developing a vision to brainstorming ideas and identifying opportunities. At some organizations, executives and employees love to develop exciting, inspiring visions. Unfortunately, sometimes these same people get stuck in their euphoria about what is possible. In these cases, the leader encourages them to identify specific opportunities to make their visions a reality.

From identifying opportunities to collecting and analyzing data. Few organizations will act on opportunities before they collect and analyze data. At some organizations, executives and employees have no trouble assessing opportunities; if anything, they enjoy collecting and analyzing data too much. At other organizations, people don't do enough analysis. They want to spring into action, without doing the appropriate amount of due diligence. The elegant leader encourages these people to collect and analyze enough information to make the best possible decision.

From collecting and analyzing data to making decisions and taking action. Some organizations are addicted to analyzing data. For instance, I worked with a nationally-recognized medical center that took a full year of analysis to decide which brand of surgical gloves to use. Whatever savings they may have generated from that decision they lost through countless management hours analyzing data. The elegant leader pushes colleagues and employees to make a decision after doing an appropriate amount of analysis—even without complete information. They know that there is no such thing as perfect, complete data.

From assigning accountability to taking action. Have you ever left a meeting in which everyone promised to do something, but never did? Leaders make sure that once people make promises, they stay accountable and take action. They do this by creating structures and systems for people to stay in touch and report progress, and by staying in continuous communication to ask about progress.

From taking action to following up and adjusting. Sometimes, employees take action and then give up. In these cases, leaders shift their focus from taking initial action steps to following up and adjusting their course. If necessary, they help people develop contingency plans. During tough times, when employees need to work extra hard to make progress, leaders are especially adept at keeping them focused on doing what's needed to get results.

From following up and adjusting to getting closure and moving on. Finally, when a project or initiative ends, leaders help people get closure. They celebrate success, identify lessons learned, clear up mistakes, and help people move on to the next challenge.

Now complete the exercise on the following page. 

Rate yourself on a scale of one to five on your skill in shifting focus to move things forward.

Self-Assessment: Shifting Focus

	Self-Rating	(1 = Needs Work;	5 = Mastery)	
Shifting from negativity to developing vision and identifying opportunities.	1	2	3	4	5
Shifting from negativity to setting goals and assigning accountability.	1	2	3	4	5
Shifting from developing a vision to brainstorming ideas and identifying opportunities.	1	2	3	4	5
Shifting from identifying opportunities to collecting and analyzing data.	1	2	3	4	5
Shifting from collecting and analyzing data to making decisions and taking action.	1	2	3	4	5
Shifting from assigning accountability to taking action.	1	2	3	4	5
Shifting from taking action to following up and adjusting.	1	2	3	4	5
Shifting from following up and adjusting to getting closure and moving on.	1	2	3	4	5

For areas where you scored less than five, what actions can you take to get better?

Think about some of your key projects and initiatives. For each initiative, where are people focusing right now? Where should they be focusing? When should they shift to a new focus? How can you help them to do that?

Do Not Give Up

When most executives quit and go home, leaders persist and move forward. Even in the face of seemingly insurmountable problems and hurdles, leaders do not give up.

Different people tend to quit at different times in the life of an initiative or goal. Some people love the thrill of starting something up, and then lose interest in following through. Others quit when they encounter the first major hurdle. Still others lose faith somewhere in the middle of an initiative, when they can't see the proverbial light at the end of the tunnel. Finally, some people quit when they are close to the end, even though all they need is one last push to succeed.

At the same time, some executives don't give up on results, but give up on other things. To succeed, they might sacrifice their personal life, their standards of quality, relationships, or even their character and integrity. To them, the end justifies the means. These are the executives who shrug at the end of a project and say, "Well, it wasn't pretty but we got the job done."

Now take the self-assessment on the following page. 

Self-Assessment: When Do You Give Up?

When in the process of moving things forward do you tend to give up? Use the checklist that follows, and check as many as apply:

- ○ At the start of an initiative, after seeing how many obstacles need to be overcome.
- ○ Just after the initial enthusiasm of creating a vision wanes.
- ○ When it comes time to make difficult decisions about priorities and resources.
- ○ When specifying goals and assigning accountability.
- ○ After taking action and encountering resistance.
- ○ Whenever boredom starts to kick in.
- ○ When it becomes time to ask others for help or advice.
- ○ In the middle of the initiative, when it becomes clear how much work is left to do.
- ○ Close to the end of an initiative, when people lack the energy to finish.
- ○ Other:

While moving things forward, which of the following, if any, have you tended to sacrifice in order to get results?

- ○ The quality of professional relationships.
- ○ Taking care of personal needs.
- ○ Using respectful and civil behavior with colleagues.
- ○ Maintaining standards of excellence and quality for internal and external customers.
- ○ Adhering to safety standards.
- ○ Having impeccable character.
- ○ Protecting the environment and health of the community.
- ○ Other:

What insights do you have about how to move things forward and not give up in the process?

Overcome Setbacks

Finally, leaders move things forward by deftly overcoming setbacks. They do this in three ways. First, they anticipate and clear obstacles. Second, they show extreme resourcefulness and creativity. Third, they cope and remain resilient as setbacks come up. This section explores each of these abilities in more detail.

Anticipate and clear obstacles. I worked with a struggling start-up that replaced its founder with a more seasoned CEO. Within three weeks, employees were raving about their new leader. He quickly secured new funding, changed the company's marketing message, and led efforts to develop a more powerful suite of products. One vice president exclaimed, "He is amazing, unstoppable. He is taking every problem we have, one by one, and solving them. It's as if he were bowling. He sees one problem, knocks it down, and then moves to the next. Soon nothing will be in our way. The former CEO was paralyzed compared to this guy."

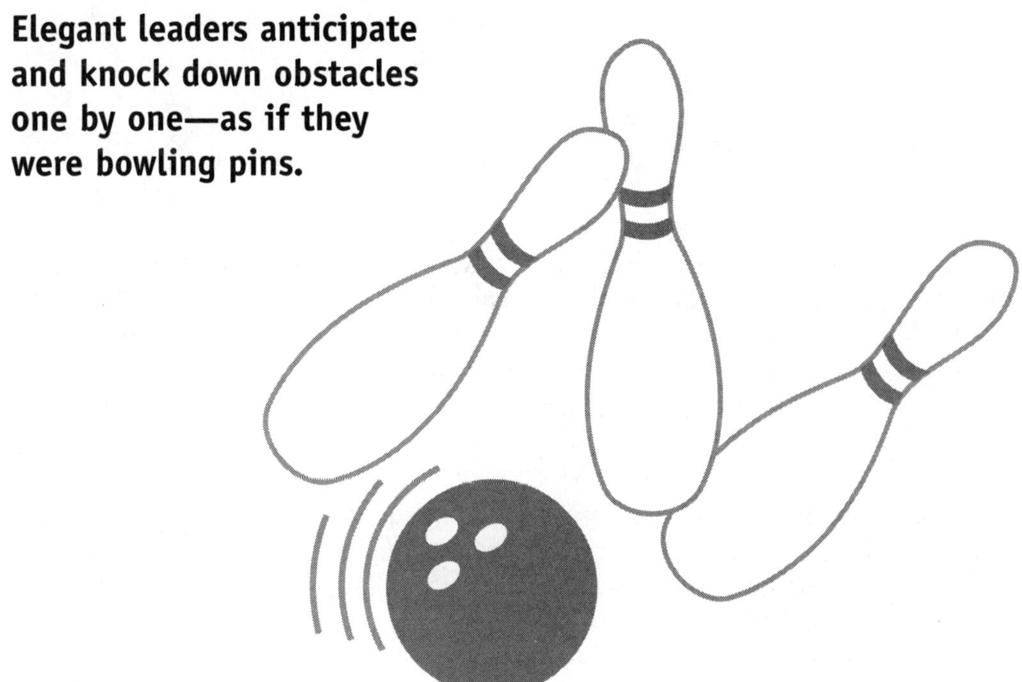

The bowling alley metaphor is an apt one for anticipating and solving problems. As an exercise, think about one of your more challenging initiatives. How well have you anticipated and addressed potential obstacles and risks? How well are you addressing current obstacles? What can you do to be like the new CEO described above?

Now complete the worksheet on the following page. 

Worksheet: Anticipating and Clearing Obstacles

Project	Current And Possible Obstacles	How You Can Address Each	By When

Be resourceful. Successful leaders are extremely resourceful. They come up with creative solutions to address significant setbacks and problems. For instance, I worked with a $350 million company that sold collector items. One week before Christmas, a shipment of heirloom-quality porcelain dolls arrived from Thailand. Of the 300 dolls in the shipment, 250 had wet dresses due to a flood on the ship. Otherwise, the dolls were fine. Meanwhile, 275 customers expected to have these dolls shipped to their homes in time for the holiday.

In order to satisfy these customers, the director of the company held a pizza party after hours. During this party, five managers in the company brought hair dryers from home and—with the director—dried the dresses until they were as good as new. For the few dresses that were not salvageable, the director went to the company's warehouse and searched until he found a stash of dolls that had been returned due to breakage. The dresses on these dolls were perfectly fine, and he used these to complete the shipment. Every customer received their order on time, and managers at the company learned about the company's commitment to service and quality.

Collector dolls might be a banal example of resourcefulness, but that's the point. Being resourceful sometimes means doing something as mundane as personally drying 250 dresses. Entrepreneurs know how to be resourceful. They know how to do outrageous things to get free publicity, convince a customer to meet with them, look big when they are tiny, and recruit other people to help them in a pinch.

Test your resourcefulness by answering these questions:

1 How could you achieve the same results if your budget were suddenly cut by 25 percent?

2 How could your organization get the same results if the size of your market (or, if you are in sales, the size of your territory) shrunk to half its present size?

3 How could your organization respond effectively if a competitor entered the market with a superior product or technology? If a competitor slashed prices by 25 percent?

4 Suppose your biggest customer threatened to switch to a competitor. How could you persuade him or her to remain loyal to you?

5 What could you do if one of your key employees chose to leave the company?

6 How big is your support network? How many different people could you call for help in a pinch?

Cope and be resilient. Finally, elegant leaders cope, and remain resilient, regardless of the setbacks they face. As Chapter Four discussed, they are comfortable swimming in the "gray zone." Coping is an important skill for leaders. In fact, one could argue that most of leadership (and management, for that matter) is about coping. The graph to the right suggests that leaders spend about 10 percent of their time on the glamorous parts of leadership: setting vision and direction, making major strategic decisions, and making daily decisions. What fills the rest of their time? Coping with daily crises, issues, and setbacks.

The majority of leadership is about coping.

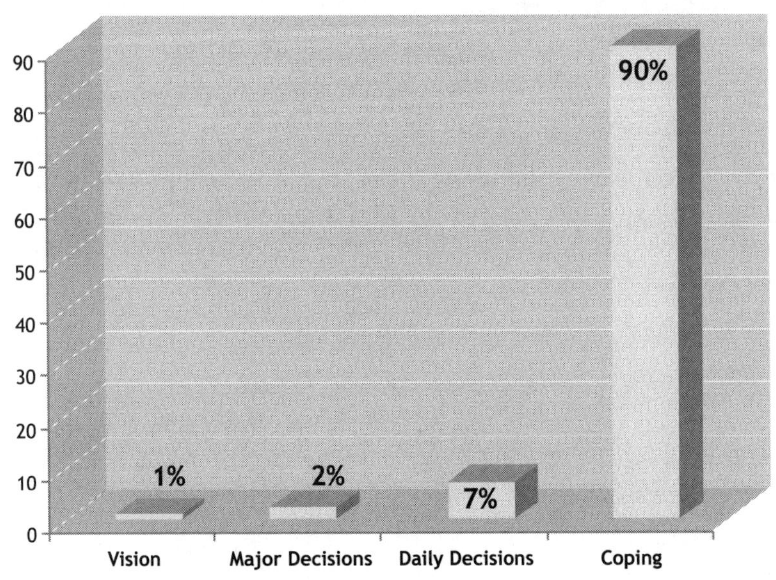

Answer the following questions about your ability to cope and be resilient:

1 What percentage of your time do you spend as a leader:

- Setting vision and direction?
- Making major strategic decisions?
- Making daily decisions?
- Coping with ongoing crises, issues, and setbacks?

2 How well do you cope? Which of the following could you do to cope better?

- ○ Change your attitude and beliefs.
- ○ Recharge by taking a vacation, working out, or some other activity.
- ○ Build a support network.
- ○ Learn to relax and remain calm.
- ○ Delegate more to other people.
- ○ Train other people to handle certain crises.
- ○ Other:
- ○ Other:

Foster Collaboration

Collaboration is the act of working with others to create opportunities and solve problems. In authentic collaboration, all parties benefit. Elegant leaders work hard to foster collaboration, both inside and outside their organizations.

Many executives find it difficult to collaborate, and prefer to do things on their own. In the short term, it may seem wiser not to collaborate with others. For instance, I worked with a chief financial officer who insisted on purchasing and installing his own financial software system, rather than involving the chief information officer. "I can do it faster, better and cheaper working on my own," he explained. "If I involve her, then I have to wait for support, and can't customize the system when I want to." Meanwhile, the CIO refused to maintain the system he chose, since he did not involve her. As a result, the CFO had to add staff in his department to maintain the system. Also, his system failed to interface effectively with the organization's manufacturing and customer relationship management systems. While he retained his freedom and independence, he cost his organization millions.

Collaborating with other organizations can be even more challenging than collaborating internally. For example, a group of non-profit organizations serving a poor neighborhood outside of San Francisco created a matrix of every non-profit in that neighborhood. They discovered over 60 organizations in this area, with significant overlap among the services provided. By collaborating, these agencies could have met the needs of the neighborhood through more coordinated services. Unfortunately, the executive directors focused more on their "turf" and on protecting their funding sources than on optimizing services to the people who needed help most.

Technology companies have learned the value of collaborating beyond the walls of their organizations. It seems that every day, a different technology company announces an alliance or partnership with another company to build a more complete product for customers, to market and distribute products more effectively, or to share technology. It is not unusual for technology companies to form alliances with competitors, competing on certain products and services, yet collaborating on others. By collaborating, they gain speed, expertise, brand recognition, and many other benefits—all of which get passed on to customers.

This section focuses on three elements of successful collaboration:

When and how to collaborate.

Break down walls within the organization.

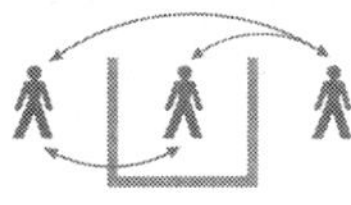

Collaborate beyond the organization's walls.

When and How to Collaborate

On paper, it is relatively simple to determine when and how to collaborate. You should collaborate when it provides more value than working alone. For collaboration to work, the benefits to both parties need to exceed the costs, as the chart below shows.

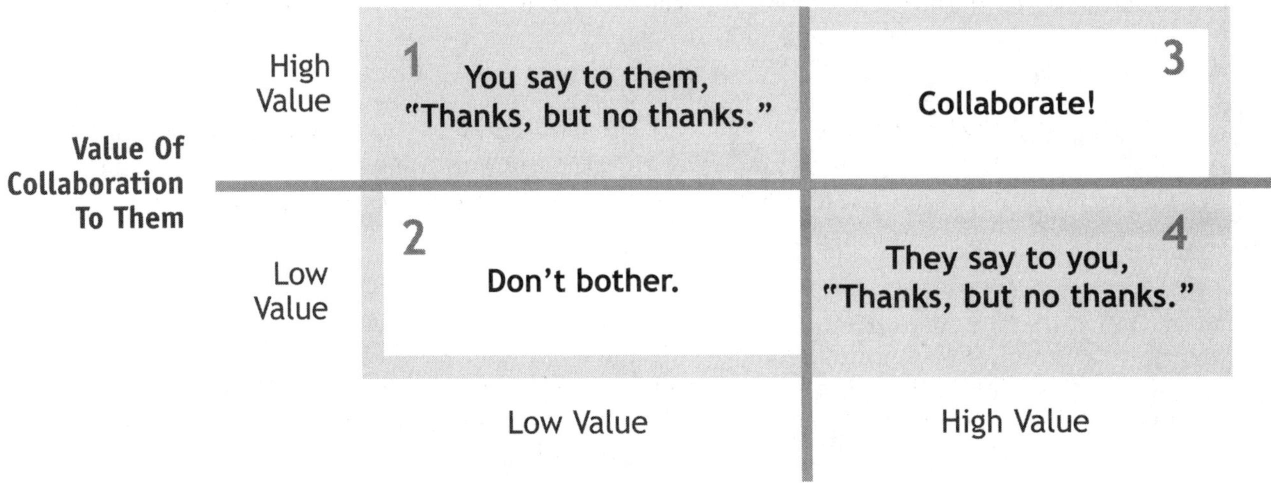

The following chart shows some of the benefits that collaboration can provide, both inside and outside the organization.

Potential Value From Collaborating Internally	Potential Value From Collaborating Externally
• Solve significant organizational problems. • Better serve customers. • Develop an advantage over the competition. • Increase speed, quality, service, and/or efficiency. • Innovate. • Share best practices. • Gain power over suppliers (e.g., by sharing information about pricing or negotiating volume discounts). • Improve internal processes.	• Increase quality and service from suppliers. • Share best practices. • Gain access to proprietary technology. • Reach customers more rapidly. • Develop new distribution channels. • Increase awareness in the marketplace by building on a larger organization's brand. • Gain scale. • Reach more profitable customers. • Develop a more complete product.

Balancing these benefits, the costs of collaborating can include the resources required to create, maintain, and improve the collaborative agreement; the risk of disclosing sensitive or proprietary information; the cost of giving up other opportunities; the risk of giving up power and control; and the vulnerability that comes from trusting colleagues outside one's immediate area. Often, despite the best intentions of all parties, these costs—especially those related to trust, power, and control—are simply too large to make collaboration feasible.

Once you decide that collaboration makes sense, you can focus on the "how." An effective collaboration requires six steps. For simple collaborations, parties can forge an agreement in as little as one meeting. For more complex collaborations, with many parties involved and lots at stake, an external mediator or facilitator can clear obstacles and move things forward.

1 ***Be explicit about the potential value of the collaboration to all parties.*** By agreeing up front on the value to everyone involved, executives can overcome inevitable rough spots that arise during discussions. They can also work together to maximize value for each other.

2 ***Be clear about what is in and out of the scope of the collaboration.*** During this step, executives should agree on boundaries and expectations. For instance, they should be open and honest about which information they will share (and won't), and about sensitive "turf" issues that are open for discussion (and not).

3 ***Explore possibilities.*** Before reaching conclusions, all parties in the collaboration should brainstorm different ways to collaborate, then explore each. This approach will create an environment for listening, mutual problem solving, and understanding each party's interests and needs in more depth.

4 ***Agree on the best solution.*** Eventually, everybody involved should agree on the best solution and arrangement for collaborating together. This agreement should include details about governance, who will do what by when, specific and measurable goals to measure success, how to monitor results, how parties will communicate, and how issues will be resolved.

5 ***Implement the plan.*** With a plan in place, the next step is to implement it, perhaps by starting with a pilot program.

6 ***Monitor results and adjust.*** Collaborations work best when everybody involved agrees to achieve specific goals and tasks. Without that, there is no way to know whether the collaboration was successful, or if you need to correct problems. Therefore, some process needs to exist to measure results and, when necessary, improve.

Now take the self-assessment on the following page. 

Answer the following questions to assess your willingness and ability to collaborate.

Self-Assessment: Collaboration

Give an example of when you have successfully collaborated inside your organization. What were the benefits of this collaboration? What were the costs? What lessons did you learn about collaborating effectively?	
Give an example of when you have successfully collaborated with people outside your organization (e.g., suppliers, channel partners, customers, competitors). What were the benefits of this collaboration? What were the costs? What lessons did you learn about collaborating effectively?	
What, if any, collaborations have your competitors forged that have given them a stronger position in the market?	
This section described a number of costs related to collaboration—especially those related to trust, vulnerability, and being willing to give up power for the greater good of the organization and customers. Which of these barriers have you encountered? How have you dealt with them?	

Break Down Walls Within the Organization

Elegant leaders work hard to break down boundaries and silos within their organizations. They do this by constantly identifying opportunities for improved communication, synchronization, and shared information among different groups.

The worksheet below provides a template for you to assess opportunities for improving collaboration among different groups in your organization. You can adapt this worksheet to fit the formal and informal relationships that exist in your organization (for instance, hospitals might want to add rows/columns for patient care, environmental services, engineering, etc.). To use the matrix, place a check mark in each box where there is room for improved collaboration between the two groups that intersect at the box. For instance, if finance and marketing have the opportunity to collaborate more effectively, mark the first open box on the matrix, where the two intersect. For areas where more than two groups could collaborate, draw connecting arrows.

	Marketing	Finance	Information Technology	Sales	R+D	Human Resources	Legal	Manufacturing	Unit 1	Unit 2
Marketing										
Finance										
Information Technology										
Sales										
R+D										
Human Resources										
Legal										
Manufacturing										
Unit 1										
Unit 2										

Now complete the worksheet on the following page.

Now that you have identified potential opportunities for improved collaboration within your organization, use the worksheet below to get specific.

Worksheet: Identify Opportunities to Collaborate Inside the Organization

Describe The Opportunity For Collaboration	Who Should Be Involved	Start Date

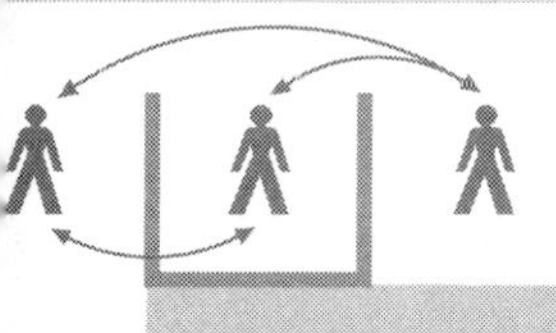

Collaborate Beyond the Organization's Walls

Organizations have enormous opportunities to collaborate more effectively with suppliers, distributors, customers, and even competitors. The following chart provides some examples.

Example: Opportunities for Collaboration Outside the Organization

Entity	Potential Opportunity
Suppliers	Decrease inventory costs. Improve quality. Increase flexibility. Standardize parts. Optimize the manufacturing process. Beta test innovative technologies. Improve the efficiency of the procurement process. Co-market.
Customers	Help them achieve the above benefits, in exchange for increased volume/loyalty.
Distributors	Gain new channels. Reach customers more quickly.
Competitors	Create a more complete product for customers. Combine proprietary technologies. Join together to advocate for new government regulations and policies.
Best practice organizations in different industries	Share best practices. Combine strengths.
Community	Create marketing opportunities by supporting community causes/events.
Other executives	Network. Get and receive support. Share ideas. Solve problems.

Now complete the worksheet on the following page. 

Given the above examples, use the following worksheet to identify potential areas for collaboration with outside organizations.

Worksheet: Identify Opportunities for Collaboration Outside the Organization

Describe The Opportunity For Collaboration	Who Should Be Involved	Start Date

Build for the Future

Recent research, especially by Jim Collins and Jerry Porras (*Built to Last: Successful Habits of Visionary Companies*), shows that great companies put structures in place to last longer than any CEO or executive. In fact, companies like General Electric® excel in their ability to create leaders like Jack Welch, time and time again.

Much of this book has focused on how you can be a better leader, and how you can achieve long-term results. This chapter now challenges you to build a legacy, an organization (or a piece of one) that will last longer than you do. Building for the future takes courage, and the rare ability to see beyond the current crisis. Few executives are successful at it.

However, those who do build for the future reap some significant benefits. First, by putting effective systems and structures in place, and by developing leaders who can take on challenging assignments, these leaders find that they have more time to focus on strategic issues. They also find that their organization becomes more valuable, because investors and potential acquirers will pay more for a company with solid structures and systems, and a deep pool of talent. Also, customers will pay more to a company that they can rely on over time—regardless of whether one key executive happens to be sick or on vacation. Finally, employees will remain at a company that enables them to grow professionally and take on increasing challenges. Companies that are built for the future become employers of choice.

This concept applies to both large and small organizations, both for-profit and non-profit. I met one entrepreneur who founded an extremely successful temporary staffing company. Within five years he had made *Inc. Magazine*'s list of America's 500 Fastest Growing Companies. Soon after, he suffered a serious skiing accident, and had to stay in bed for nine months. During that time without him, revenue dropped, profits disappeared, and he almost lost his business. When he recovered, he decided to train his employees to become leaders who could run the business without him. Today, his business is extremely profitable, and he spends significantly less time working than he did before his accident.

This chapter provides seven strategies to help you build for the future:

Assess the current strength of the organization. This section provides an assessment that will show you where you need to focus to strengthen your organization.

Delegate to develop leaders and give you more time. Leaders give people more and more responsibility, both to develop a pool of talent, and to be able to focus on more strategic issues. This section provides a simple tool to help you do that.

Identify and meet strategic leadership needs. This section offers a tool for identifying the key capabilities you need in your organization and how to develop them—whether through internal assignments and training, or by recruiting from outside.

Tell stories that will teach employees how to lead. This section offers a number of story topics that every leader should develop in order to teach others to lead.

Teach employees to lead through dialogue. Strong organizations engage all employees in dialogue about strategy, key issues, and goals. That way, leaders develop emerging leaders through daily conversations about the future. This section offers a series of questions that can start productive dialogues to strengthen your organization.

Create systems to build a strong organization. Strong organizations have effective systems. This section provides a comprehensive tool to help you assess the systems you have in place today, and the systems you need to develop or improve.

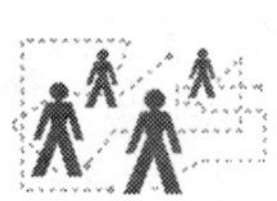

Create a nimble, resilient, high-performance culture. Through their decisions, actions, and language, leaders create the culture of their organization. This section challenges you to think about your culture, and how you can make it more effective.

Assess the Current Strength of Your Organization

The following questions will help you assess the systems and structures of your organization. After answering each question, add up your totals.

Self-Assessment: Current Ability of Your Organization to Last

		No	Yes
1	If I suddenly left the organization, I trust that it would continue to thrive without me.	○	○
2	I have given, and continue to give, key managers and executives more control of the organization.	○	○
3	I frequently give key executives and managers challenging assignments to help them develop as leaders, and to lighten my workload.	○	○
4	I have identified, and begun to groom, one or more possible successors within the organization.	○	○
5	If I suddenly left the organization, key executives and managers would continue to set and achieve aggressive goals.	○	○
6	If I suddenly left the organization, our standards of quality and service would remain as high as or higher than they are now.	○	○
7	If I suddenly left the organization, key executives and managers would proactively identify, and respond effectively to, changes in the market.	○	○
8	If I suddenly left the organization, I could rely on key executives and managers to continue to develop an effective strategic plan, and a budget to support the plan.	○	○
9	If I suddenly left the organization, I could rely on key executives and managers to execute the strategic plan and budget already in place.	○	○
10	If I suddenly left the organization, I could rely on key executives and managers to strengthen the company for the future, while still achieving aggressive short-term goals.	○	○
11	The current executive and management team understands and agrees with the vision and strategic direction of the organization.	○	○
12	All employees in the organization clearly understand our current strategy, as well as the vision for where the organization is going.	○	○
13	Front-line staff respect, trust, and respond effectively to our managers and key executives—without my oversight.	○	○

		No	Yes
14	Key customers are loyal to the organization, not to me.	○	○
15	The organization has systems in place to reward top performers and remove mediocre performers, with or without my oversight.	○	○
16	I have systematically taken the knowledge "in my head" about our products, processes, and best practices, and created systems so that everyone in the organization can access this knowledge.	○	○
17	I spend at least 25 percent of my time coaching and developing emerging leaders.	○	○
18	Words that describe the organization's culture include: *results-oriented, nimble,* and *resilient*.	○	○
19	The organization operates with a strong set of values, and hires and evaluates employees based partly on their adherence to those values.	○	○
20	The organization has a proactive strategy and process to continually hire, train, develop, and challenge leaders. For instance, each manager and executive completes a development plan detailing goals for improvement and how to achieve them. Similarly, the organization offers leaders a career path that allows them to run part of the business.	○	○
	TOTAL		

How did you do? What insights did you have about the strength of your organization, and whether it would thrive, survive, or dive without you?

The assessment looks at a number of areas:

- ***Your own willingness and ability to trust your people***
  (especially questions 1, 2, and 3—and to some degree 7, 8, 9, 13, and 14);
- ***How well you develop leaders in your organization***
  (especially questions 2, 3, 4, 5, 7, 8, 9, 10, 17, and 20);
- ***How well you have put systems in place to create an effective organization***
  (especially questions 4, 5, 6, 8, 10, 12, 15, 16, and 20); and
- ***How well you have created a performance-oriented culture***
  (especially questions 5, 6, 10, 11, 12, 13, 15, 18, and 19).

This section continues on the following page. 

As you review the assessment and think about steps you can take to strengthen your organization, watch out for some common traps:

Lack of trust. Some leaders do not give up control of their organization because they do not trust their key people. They explain, "I'd like to hand this off to my team, but I am not ready." When leaders commit to training and teaching their team to take on greater responsibilities, they often become impatient with the time it takes to transfer their knowledge. Why surround yourself with people you do not trust? Either replace your team with people you do trust, or take the time to develop your current team.

Looking for the perfect person to solve your problems. Many leaders respond to the survey by saying, "I'm not concerned. All I need to do is recruit someone who can lead the organization." While this approach might help build your team, hiring a new key executive rarely creates a more lasting organization. Rather, it tends to perpetuate the problem of having an organization that relies on key people rather than on enduring systems and structures.

Ego gratification. Some leaders enjoy being the person that rushes in to fight fires, solve other people's problems, and be the hero. Even though they acknowledge that this approach costs them personal freedom, satisfaction, and the long-term viability of their organization, they don't take the necessary steps to change their situation. They have a range of excuses, but really, they enjoy being the key person. For them, building a lasting organization will never be a priority until they either feel too much pain from fighting fires all day, or acknowledge that the benefits of building a lasting organization outweigh the payoff of being the hero.

Short-term focus. Finally, some executives doubt that building a lasting organization makes any sense. When times are good, they pay themselves a terrific bonus and declare a huge dividend. When times are bad, they lay off staff. To them, thinking about building for the future is irrelevant. That's fine, if they are willing to sacrifice the additional benefits of building a lasting organization: greater valuation on sale, better customer loyalty and brand recognition, ability to charge higher prices, and ultimately—for some—greater satisfaction and fulfillment.

Assuming that you have managed to avoid these traps, what opportunities exist to strengthen your organization for the future? Use the worksheet on the following page to write down some ideas.

Worksheet: Opportunities to Strengthen for the Future

Opportunity	Specific Action Or Initiative	By When

Delegate to Develop Leaders and Give You Time

Many leaders could have more time—and develop other leaders—by taking a rigorous look at how they spend their day. With that data in hand, they could quickly identify opportunities to delegate all or some of their work to others. As a result, emerging leaders could develop new capabilities by taking on new responsibilities. Also, the leader will have more time to spend on new projects or on personal activities.

How long has it been since you took an inventory of how you spend your time? As an exercise, record everything you do during a week, in 15-minute intervals. Then, total the numbers in the worksheet on the following page. How many hours in each category could you have delegated to somebody else? Who? What specifically could you have delegated to them? What would you need to do to train them?

Based on this exercise, how much time can you save? I worked with a bank CEO who found that he could save an hour a week by having somebody else answer calls requesting permission to send him solicitations. Likewise, I worked with an entrepreneur who cut her hours down from 60 per week to 40 (and spent the extra 20 hours per week with her children) by delegating marketing and administrative activities to her employees.

Everybody wins with this exercise—if you are willing to take the time to do it, and if you are willing to delegate work to others.

Worksheet: Opportunities to Delegate

Process/ Function	Hours Per Week Of Your Time Spent On This Process/ Function	Hours Per Week Spent That You Could Delegate	To Whom You Could Delegate This Work	Specific Work Or Assignments You Could Delegate	What It Would Take To Hand Off And Train
Strategy					
Planning					
Budgeting and forecasting					
Finance					
Marketing					
Sales					
Recruiting					
Other human resources functions					
Serving customers					
R+D/ Product development					
Developing leaders					
Other:					
Other:					
Other:					

Identify and Meet Strategic Leadership Needs

Leaders create other leaders. That way, they have plenty of people who can help build and strengthen the organization, and who can take over after they leave. Leaders create leaders by assigning them challenging work, and by creating systems and structures that enhance their development.

Creating leaders isn't part of a fuzzy, vague process. Rather, leadership development flows from your strategic needs. Based on the anticipated strategic needs of your organization in the future (and perhaps the present), you can identify the key capabilities you will need. You can then plan to develop those capabilities, either by working with in-house employees, or by recruiting those capabilities from outside the organization.

This section provides you with a series of questions that will help you identify and fill your leadership development needs.

Worksheet: Identify and Meet Strategic Leadership Needs

1 What are the key strategic needs of the organization over the next couple of years?

2 What key capabilities do your leaders need to have in order to meet these needs?

3 What capabilities are required to meet your current strategic challenges?

4 What capabilities are required in the organization in order for you to become less critical to the organization's success, and for other people to take more significant leadership roles?

5 For capabilities that you listed in the previous questions, think about the capabilities that your current executives and managers do not already possess. Plan how you can begin developing these capabilities today by:

a Assigning key people to new projects that will develop them:

Assignment	To Whom	How To Train	By When

b Providing internal mentors to teach people critical knowledge and skills, and to help employees plan for their long-term development:

Who Will Be Mentored	Who Will Be The Mentor	Topic(s)	By When

c Contracting for external consulting and coaching:

Key Capability	Consulting/Coaching Firm	By When

d Providing formal education and training:

Key Capability	Who Will Be Trained	How	By When

e Recruiting from outside the organization:

Capability Needed	New Role	Target Start Date

Tell Stories that Teach Employees to Lead

As was noted earlier in this book, a number of management and leadership scholars have identified storytelling as a key tool that leaders use. People love stories. Stories help people to learn and remember, while entertaining them. Stories also provide leaders with a great method for teaching others how to lead, and offer a simple strategy for strengthening the organization.

This section suggests a number of different story topics. Which ones would be useful teaching tools right now?

Pick a few from the worksheet on the following page, and prepare some stories that will teach and inspire others to lead.

Worksheet: Tell Stories

1 What does it take to succeed in your line of work? Tell a story about how you developed each of those skills, and the first time you used each successfully (or learned from a failure about how to improve).

2 Tell a story about a time you beat the competition against all odds (or about lessons learned from losing to them).

3 Tell a story about overcoming, or surviving during, an economic downturn.

4 Tell a story about a key strategic decision.

5 Tell a story about recruiting and developing great people.

6 Tell a story that demonstrates how to successfully manage the finances of the organization (or how not to do it).

7 Tell a story about somebody who performed an extraordinary act to serve a customer (or about a lesson learned from poor customer service).

8 Tell a story that illustrates the importance of your organization's planning process, and how to navigate the process.

9 Tell a story about one or more key moments in the company's evolution.

10 Tell a story about how the company developed one or more of its top products. Tell a story about an unsuccessful product, and lessons learned.

11 Tell a story that celebrates the unique talents of somebody in the organization.

12 Tell a story about an employee who exemplifies the values of the organization.

13 Tell a story that helps to explain the organization's unique culture.

14 Tell a story about someone who set and achieved an "impossible" goal for the company.

15 Tell a story about one or more key achievements of the organization's current leaders, and what got them into their current position.

16 Tell a story about an employee who didn't make the grade and had to leave the company (and what that means about the company's standards).

Teach People to Lead Through Dialogue

In addition to telling stories, another way that leaders teach others to lead is by engaging people in a challenging dialogue about possibilities and opportunities at the organization. This kind of dialogue trains people to think about the business for themselves, instead of relying on the leader for answers. When done with respect for the people involved, and in the spirit of a true inquiry, it also increases employee commitment and involvement in the company's success. Most importantly, dialogue can lead to some great answers and ideas that the leader would never have thought of alone.

The way to start a challenging dialogue is by asking a challenging question. Following are examples of four types of questions that you can use to engage others in dialogue. First, questions that begin with "What if" invite discussion about potential situations or crises, and the best way to handle them. Second, strategic questions challenge people to think more clearly and critically about the best strategic course for the company, or a piece of it, to pursue. Third, questions about how to achieve remarkable goals set high expectations, and push people to go beyond what they might think is possible. Finally, as Collins and Porras note in *Built to Last*, questions that encourage people to shift from "either/or" and "but" to "and" enable them to think more creatively about possibilities.

Examples of "What if" questions:

- What would we do if a new competitor entered our market with twice as much capital as we have, and began an aggressive advertising campaign designed to take market share away from us?
- What would we do if a competitor came out with a product or service that competed directly with one of our products, but at half the price?
- What would we do if one of our products or services became obsolete overnight?
- What would we do if a key employee left?
- What would we do if our budget was cut in half, but our revenue goals remained the same?

Examples of strategic questions:

- What do we do better than anybody else in our market?
- What will happen in the market over the next three years?
- How big could our revenue and market share get?
- Who are our target customers? Does this make sense?
- Which customers should we delight?
- Which customers should we fire?
- What strengths can we build on?
- What competitive weaknesses can we target?

Examples of questions that challenge people to achieve remarkable goals:

- How can we improve quality 50 percent?
- How can we achieve the same revenue with half the marketing cost?
- How can we introduce a new product in half the time?

Examples of questions that shift people from "either/or" and "but" to "and":

- How can we reduce costs and improve quality and service?
- How can we achieve short-term goals and do what it will take to achieve our five-year vision?
- How can we develop this new product and still provide support and maintenance on our current products?
- How can we expand globally and still retain a local feel?

Once you begin the dialogue, your job as the leader is to probe, offer other perspectives and points of view, and build on interesting answers. You should not assume you know the answer, but rather help people think more deeply about the issues.

Given the above examples, and your own organizational issues, what questions will you ask to help engage your people in dialogue?

Worksheet: Questions to Engage Employees in Dialogue

"What If" Questions	Strategic Questions	Questions About How To Achieve Remarkable Goals	Questions That Shift From "Either/Or" To "And"

Create Systems to Build a Strong Organization

Strong systems create a strong organization. Systems range from solid strategic planning and budgeting processes to systems to develop and reward top performers. This section provides a tool for identifying which systems to strengthen or put in place in your company.

What can you do to improve the following systems and processes so that the organization can function without you? See the completed example first for ideas.

Example: Put Systems in Place to Build a Strong Organization

Systems And Processes	Improvement (Illustrative)
Strategic planning	Develop a formal strategic planning process, including a language and way of thinking about strategy. Coach and challenge the executive team to think more strategically. Send the executive and management team to a training session on strategic thinking. Interview the entire company for their views about what our strategy should be, and involve them in the planning process.
Budgeting	Create an open-book management system. Train all employees to understand how to read and manage the budget. Create incentives to ensure that all employees receive bonuses based on meeting the plan.
Providing outstanding customer service	Train all managers to be able to train staff on customer service. Survey customers quarterly, and have all managers meet with each customer monthly.
Developing strong relationships with customers	Take executives and managers on sales and service calls. Coach them on specific techniques and strategies to develop long-term relationships. Create a monthly meeting to discuss case studies. Develop a methodology for thinking more strategically about customer relationships.
Developing new products	Set goals for new product development during the next fiscal year. Assign a team to write case studies on successful product development in the past.
Improving quality and service	Teach all managers TQM processes. Set goals as part of the annual bonus requirement.
Forming and nurturing strategic alliances	Take two top executives on calls when forming alliances. Begin to hand off relationships to them over the next six months.
Creating a vision	Let our chief operating officer lead the visioning process this year by using a collaborative and facilitative process. Have her take training on this subject.
Managing cash flow	Train all employees to understand the importance of cash flow through open-book management processes, as noted above.

Systems And Processes	Improvement (Illustrative)
Optimizing the capital structure	Assign the chief financial officer the role of proposing the optimal capital structure, and of training the controller to become proficient in this area.
Managing profit and loss	Give three managers profit-and-loss responsibility and authority. Create an incentive program. Develop a reporting structure so that the CEO can work directly with them.
Communicating with front-line staff	Human resources will create a process to ensure that all employees understand the goals, the budget, and the strategy—as well as key developments in meeting goals and serving customers.
Installing appropriate information technology	Install new software for managing customer relationships.
Managing performance and professional development	Create a formal training and development curriculum for managers and executives. Revise the review process to be based on results, not just a subjective evaluation by supervisors.
Rewarding top performers	Create a recognition and bonus program for employees who excel in revenue generation, product development, and profit management.
Removing mediocre performers	Create a process to identify and remove employees in the lowest 10 percent. Include a probationary period for improvement.
Recruiting leaders	Recruit three new employees who have the potential to build $10 million businesses.
Developing leaders	Create a leadership program for top managers and executives to teach them about the company's history, direction, investors, and board. Rotate executives so that each understands the entire business. Create two or three career "tracks" that emerging leaders can follow in order to grow professionally, and help build the company.
Assigning work	Where possible, assign work based on profit accountability, not on tasks.
Managing knowledge	Create a knowledge-management system to capture lessons learned about three areas: building relationships with key clients, developing products, and targeting new prospects.

Now complete the worksheet on the following page. 

Worksheet: Put Systems in Place to Build a Strong Organization

Systems And Processes	Improvement	Who/By When
Strategic planning		
Budgeting		
Providing outstanding customer service		
Developing strong relationships with customers		
Developing new products		
Improving quality and service		
Forming and nurturing strategic alliances		
Creating a vision		
Managing cash flow		
Optimizing the capital structure		
Managing profit and loss		
Communicating with front-line staff		
Installing appropriate information technology		
Managing performance and professional development		
Rewarding top performers		
Removing mediocre performers		
Recruiting leaders		
Developing leaders		
Assigning work		
Managing knowledge		

Create a Nimble, High-Performance Culture

The final way you can strengthen your organization is by working constantly to develop a culture that is nimble, resilient, and that focuses on achieving outstanding performance. As a leader in your organization, you have a significant say—if not the primary say—in the norms, decision-making, and values of the organization. Your actions and words set the tone. Therefore, if you want to change your culture, change your behaviors.

You can develop a nimble culture by:

- Teaching employees how to make rapid, accurate decisions.
- Teaching employees how to embrace change—before a crisis forces change.
- Encouraging open and honest communication.
- Encouraging collaboration and information sharing.
- Putting in place information systems that provide real-time data, so that people can make real-time decisions.
- Giving people as much authority and responsibility as they can handle, if not more.

You can develop a resilient culture by:

- Modeling resilience by bouncing back during your own setbacks.
- Remaining an unflappable source of optimism, support, and strength.
- Encouraging innovation, risk-taking, and learning from mistakes.
- Encouraging people to put the past in the past and move into the future.

You can develop a performance-oriented culture by:

- Continuously raising standards.
- Setting aggressive goals.
- Refusing to tolerate mediocrity.
- Rewarding top performers and removing average performers.
- Telling people when they do not meet your expectations, and providing suggestions on ways to improve.
- Hiring the best.
- Giving people challenging assignments and the tools they need to succeed.

Based on the above advice, what are two or three ways in which you could do a better job creating a nimble, resilient, high-performance culture?

1

2

3

Give Something Back

Elegant leaders give back to their communities, perhaps out of altruism, or simply to fulfill a desire to share what they have gained. However, many who give back find that they reap significant personal rewards by serving, such as: meeting people, becoming part of a cause or issue that inspires them, promoting their organization, making business contacts, and benefitting from the positive changes they make.

This final chapter provides ideas for using your good fortune, talents, and resources to make a positive difference beyond your organization. A lot is at stake. A groundbreaking study by Robert Putnam, author of *Bowling Alone*, shows a significant decline in involvement in civic activities over the last few decades. At the same time, many communities express concern about and resentment toward profitable organizations and wealthy individuals who don't seem to contribute beyond the taxes that we all pay. The more you set an example and encourage others to do the same, the more we can improve our communities and develop future civic leaders.

While this chapter tends to describe "community" as the town or city where you live, the word has a much broader meaning. It means any formal or informal network of relationships that interests you (e.g., the business community, Harvard graduates, the softball league, etc.) At the same time, if you can, you are also encouraged to give back on a state, national and global scale.

The pages that follow explore four themes of giving back:

Understand first, then get involved. The issues facing our society are complex, with numerous constituents and points of view. What works in our organizations might backfire in the communities we choose to serve. Elegant leaders take time to understand the issues that matter to them, before intruding with their point of view.

Choose areas of personal interest. Don't give back to a cause only because you think you should. Instead, find issues and opportunities that inspire you, interest you, and satisfy your personal aspirations and goals.

Identify opportunities to serve while promoting your organization. Giving back can also be a smart marketing strategy. Numerous organizations gain visibility and good will in their community by wisely combining marketing and publicity with service.

Encourage employees and colleagues to serve. Many employees would love to have the time and support of their employer to contribute in their communities. Also, by encouraging everyone in your organization to give back in ways that matter to them, you can engage and develop future leaders.

Understand First, Then Get Involved

Before giving back, it is essential to understand the issues that you want to resolve—especially when they involve your community. Community issues can be extremely complex, with numerous constituents, allegiances, points of view, interconnections, and history. The people involved in community issues often come from many different backgrounds, with different leadership styles, assumptions, agendas, and degrees of flexibility. In fact, the complexity and chaos in most organizations pales in comparison to that of our communities.

Fortunately, aside from reading the local newspaper, there are a number of ways to understand community issues. Many towns and cities offer leadership programs that teach aspiring leaders about the history and complexity of their locale. Service clubs, like Rotary and Lions, feature speeches from leaders at their meetings. You can join committees at your chamber of commerce, apply for positions on citizen advisory boards, and/or join the board of a non-profit organization.

The following worksheet lists a large number of issues. Assess your understanding of those that interest you, then answer the questions that follow.

Worksheet: Understand the Issues

Area Or Issue	Assess Your Understanding Of The Area Or Issue
Overall issues facing your local community	
How the business community organizes and works	
How local, state and federal government works	
How the non-profit sector works	
Environmental issues	
Health issues	
Human needs and social service issues	
Educational issues	
Diversity issues (e.g., women, minorities)	
Taxation issues	

Area Or Issue	Assess Your Understanding Of The Area Or Issue
Youth issues	
The arts	
Entertainment	
Religion and spirituality	
Building community and relationships (e.g., parades, local gatherings)	
Transportation issues	
Housing issues	
Economic development issues	
Crime and safety issues	
Aging issues	
Sports and recreation	
Knowing the neighbors	
Other:	

Now answer the questions on the following page.

Now answer these questions:

1 Which of the issues interest you the most?

2 How can you learn more about these issues? Who can help you get more involved?

3 What organizations can you join to get a broader perspective about your community, its issues, and how it works?

Choose Areas of Personal Interest

Some leaders give back out of guilt or shame. Others believe that they have to contribute money like Bill Gates, or volunteer like Mother Theresa. On the contrary, this section suggests that you get involved and give back on a scale and in a way that inspires and nurtures you. For instance, the founder of the Surfriders Foundation, an extremely successful non-profit group dedicated to preserving our oceans, formed the organization partly to support his love for surfing. Most non-profit board members join boards either because they feel passionately about the organization's mission, or because they want to meet people in their community—not because they feel they should. Some of the happiest community activists coach soccer, organize neighborhood barbeques, join Sisterhood at their local congregation, or form community carpools. The secret is to find a way of giving back that is mutually beneficial.

Choosing an issue or organization that inspires you will increase your chances of making a real and positive difference. Given your work in the previous section, use the following worksheet to determine specifically how you will give back. What issue or area of interest will you address? How will you contribute (e.g., joining a board or an organization, convening experts and leaders, organizing an event, volunteering time and expertise, giving money, writing letters, etc.)?
By when?

Worksheet: Identify Areas of Personal Interest

Issue/Area Of Interest	How You Want To Contribute	Next Step/By When

Serve While Promoting Your Organization

Just as you can give back to support your personal interests, you can also give back in a way that promotes your organization. Many civic and non-profit groups provide sponsorships that can result in significant recognition for your organization. In fact, some companies make serving their community an integral part of their marketing strategy. They support local arts organizations, participate in parades, create scholarships, and provide volunteers—all in exchange for visibility and good will in the community. In my county, a local real-estate brokerage firm has become quite visible by addressing the needs of the homeless. The leading community bank hosts an event to recognize voluntary leaders who represent the spirit of the community. If your organization is large enough, it can support local, state and even national causes.

In the worksheet below, identify opportunities for your organization to contribute that will also increase visibility and promote good will.

Worksheet: Opportunities to Contribute While Promoting Your Organization

Area Or Issue	Opportunities To Contribute To The Area Or Issue While Promoting Your Organization
Environmental issues	
Health issues	
Human needs and social service issues	
Educational issues	
Diversity issues (e.g., women, minorities)	
Youth issues	
The arts	
Entertainment	

Area Or Issue	Opportunities To Contribute To The Area Or Issue While Promoting Your Organization
Religion and spirituality	
Local parades, galas, celebrations, fairs, and other events	
Transportation issues	
Housing issues	
Economic development issues	
Crime and safety issues	
Aging issues	
Sports and recreation	
Other:	

Encourage Employees and Colleagues to Serve

Giving back not only provides personal fulfillment and potential opportunities to promote your organization, it can also be a way to engage and develop employees. Opportunities to serve can help future leaders develop essential skills and become visible to other leaders (and potential customers). At the same time, many employees appreciate opportunities to serve and lead in their communities, and may remain more loyal to employers that encourage them to do so.

On the following worksheet, record ideas that you have to encourage employees and colleagues in your organization to give something back.

Worksheet: Encouraging Your Employees and Colleagues to Serve

Opportunities To Serve	Ideas To Encourage Employees And Colleagues To Serve
Serving on non-profit boards	
Joining and participating in service organizations (e.g., Rotary)	
Volunteering time and expertise—individually or with a team	
Participating on citizen advisory committees	
Participating actively in chamber(s) of commerce or like groups	
Completing local civic awareness/leadership programs	
Creating a volunteer/community leadership program within the organization	
Promoting philanthropy	
Launching an initiative to improve some aspect of the community	
Other:	

Conclusion

Elegant leaders keep learning, keep raising the bar, and keep getting better—so while this book might have a conclusion, the practice of elegant leadership never does. Simplicity, power, practicality, and gracefulness are all sliding scales.

If you have completed the exercises in each chapter of this book, then you have truly accomplished a lot. You have taken steps to change any disagreeable behaviors, shifted your attitude, developed a simple and compelling strategy, strengthened relationships, improved your ability to communicate powerfully, enhanced your ability to influence others and move things forward, expanded the way you think about problems, fostered collaboration, and developed your organization for the future.

After all of that work, this is a good time to focus, to get grounded again. While Chapter One provided a dashboard to remind you of your priorities (and might be good to revisit), this conclusion provides three final exercises. As you complete each one, hone in on the essential answers that will make the biggest difference to yourself, and to the people you lead.

Exercises: Conclusion

What are three things that you must do going forward to succeed in your career and help your organization to succeed?

1
2
3

What are three ways that you can continue to improve and develop as an elegant leader in your chosen field?

1
2
3

What are three things that you can do immediately to raise the standards and expectations you have of yourself, your colleagues, and/or your organization?

1
2
3

This book is meant to serve as a reference. You never really finish it. I hope that you pick it up frequently, review the chapters that call to you, and continue to master the practice of elegant leadership.

Please keep me informed about your progress, challenges, setbacks, and results: aneitlich@sagogroup.com.

Bibliography

Collins, James C. and Jerry I. Porras. *Built to Last: Successful Habits of Visionary Companies.* HarperCollins Publishers, 1997.

Gardner, Howard E. *Leading Minds: An Anatomy of Leadership.* Basic Books, 1996.

Leonard, George. *Mastery: The Keys to Success and Long-Term Fulfillment.* Plume Books, 1991.

Putnam, Robert D. *Bowling Alone: The Collapse and Revival of American Community.* Simon & Schuster Books, 2000.

Tichy, Noel M. *The Leadership Engine: How Winning Companies Build Leaders at Every Level.* HarperCollins Publishers, 1997.

Wheatley, Margaret J. *Leadership and the New Science: Discovering Order in a Chaotic World.* Berrett-Koehler Publishers, 1999.

About the Author

Andrew Neitlich is the founder and president of The Sago Group (www.sagogroup.com), a consulting firm focused on strategy and organizational development. Entrepreneurs and executives come to him to clarify their strategy and goals, develop new capabilities, engage and mobilize colleagues, and strengthen their organizations. His unique coaching and consulting model gets results rapidly and elegantly.

Since 1994, he has consulted with and coached executives at leading organizations, helping them become more effective leaders, formulate strategy, improve productivity, increase revenues, and develop high-performance cultures. He has led the training and professional development arm of a major management consulting firm. He also built and led a strategic marketing practice for a leading Silicon Valley consulting firm. From this experience, he created a coaching and consulting practice that fuses the best practices of strategic management consulting, organizational development, facilitation, and executive education.

Andrew writes, speaks, and consults on a variety of topics, including leadership, influence, customer loyalty, strategic thinking, coaching skills for executives, communicating powerfully, and building strong organizations. He has also produced a television series featuring interviews with leaders in the San Francisco Bay Area.

Andrew received his MBA from Harvard Business School, and a BA in Anthropology *summa cum laude* from Harvard College. He lives in Marin County, California with his family.